Till Death Us Do Part

Till Death Us Do Part

Building a Healthy Marriage

J. John

Authentic

First published 2004 by Authentic Media, 9 Holdom Avenue,
Bletchley, Milton Keynes, Bucks, MK1 1QR, UK and PO Box
1047, Waynesboro, GA 30830-2047, USA.

The material in this book was first published as
part of *Marriage Works* by J. John in 2002 by
Authentic Media.

British Library Cataloguing in Publication Data
A catalogue record for this book is available from the British
Library.

1-86024-465-3

Cover design by David Lund
Print Management by Adare Carwin
Printed and Bound in Denmark by Nørhaven Paperback

I dedicate this book to my best friend, my beloved,
and the mother of my three sons –
KILLY

Thank you for making my life the happy
adventure that it is.

Contents

Acknowledgements

The idea for a book on marriage came from Katharine Draper, my faithful PA. Thank you, Katharine, for your inspirational challenge to me.

I also want to thank Paul Wilson, my colleague, who has faithfully supported me in all the Philo Trust projects I undertake. Further thanks are also due to the trustees of the Philo Trust, under whose auspices I carry out my work: Terry and Juanita Baker, Jamie Colman, Bob Fuller, Mike Carson and Peter Wright, I appreciate and value your wisdom and guidance.

I'd like to thank those friends who read various drafts of this manuscript and who asked stimulating questions and made helpful suggestions. I am very grateful to Julie Bignell, Fi Costa, Sue Da Costa, Edie Gould, Jane Hastings, Killy John, Barbara Marsh and Alison Walley. The reason why I asked so many women to comment was to counteract any masculine bias. I think it worked!

I also want to thank all the staff at Authentic who have been involved with this project, especially Graham Williams, the Managing Director, and Malcolm Down, the Publishing Manager, for their support, encouragement and enthusiasm.

Introduction

I try to listen to people. As someone who does a lot of speaking, I have to. After all, if you don't listen, you end up giving answers to questions that no one is asking. And whenever I listen to people today, I seem to detect a common and recurring issue – a concern about marriage.

This concern doesn't just come from the disturbing official statistics on marital breakdown, it comes from the fact that we all personally know, and know closely, marriages that have failed and failed painfully. Some of us have been in failed marriages; others of us have been close enough to be hit by the fall-out from them. And what worries us is that some of the marriages that we have watched fail have not been the light-hearted, tentative ventures of totally incompatible people that you just knew would never work – they have been serious and promising unions between apparently ideal matches.

The result has been a tremendous and widespread crisis of confidence in marriage. Twenty years ago, a newly-wed couple expected their marriage to work and dared to hope that it would be great. Now, a couple getting married expect their marriage to hit trouble and only dare to hope that it will work. This climate of doubt and unease affects all marriages. Being married today is like driving along a motorway and passing traffic accident after traffic accident. After a while you begin to wonder whether you will be next. Even in marriages that are working well, there is now a lingering unease – will it last?

Inevitably too, as the number of failed marriages increases, so the number of marriages that are doing well goes down. Increasingly, people are growing up without any models of successful marriages to look to. They grew up in broken families, their friends come from broken families and the idea of a permanent, stable and joyful marriage is something that they can only dream of. In fact, some of them are beginning to suspect that the whole concept of a happy marriage is just a myth. And because such cynicism is self-fulfilling, it predictably breeds new marital disasters.

I have written this book because so many people have hurts and questions relating to marriage. It seems to me that here, in the area of marriage, the need for help, advice and encouragement is great.

Who This Book Is For

This book is written for those who are married (whether happily or unhappily). Actually, the only qualification needed for reading this book is this: you must want your marriage to work. If you are married and you want out, then this book is not for you. After all, if you don't really want a marriage to work, then nothing I write can make it work. This book is for those that are trying to make marriage work.

Now here I want to say a bit about where I am coming from. Whether they try to hide it or not, all writers on marriage are affected by their own experiences. So, for example, few people who have been through a divorce write books extolling the virtues of marriage, and many of the sour, angry books on marriage come out of sour and angry marriages. Some writings on marriage are, frankly, little more than exercises in self-justification along the lines of 'the reason my marriage didn't work is because the institution of marriage can't work'. So, at the start, let me come clean – I am positive about marriage. I am positive for two reasons: because I have experienced a good marriage and because, as a Christian, I believe that human beings were designed with the potential to be married.

Let me say something about both of those reasons. With regard to my own marriage: I have been married to Killy for 21 years and we have three sons. Killy[1] is my best friend and I am more in love with Killy today than when I married her on 23 July 1983. My three sons, Michael, Simeon and Benjamin, are a joy and are not only my sons, but also my dearest friends. I find parenting hard work – I think by the time you get the hang of parenting your children have left home!

With regard to the Christian perspective, I want to say that anything written on marriage is affected not only by the writer's experiences but also by the writer's beliefs and values. Whether a writer openly states it or not, their faith – whether it is Buddhism, Christianity or atheism – affects what they write on marriage. There is simply no neutral position. My own position then, is that of being a practising Christian. Actually, as our ideas of marriage in Britain are still overwhelmingly influenced by the Christian tradition, that is quite a helpful background to come from.

Now, having said that, let me reassure any reader who

---

[1] Killy's comment on reading the first draft of this book was 'It's a shame we didn't have this when we got married!'

is not a Christian. The first is that you don't have to be a Christian to read this book. I have tried hard to avoid any jargon or concepts that may be unfamiliar, and as I have written this I have tried to keep in mind someone who has never opened a Bible or attended a church service. What I have written here is free for you to take and use, whether you are a Christian or not. Of course, if you find it helpful then you might well decide that Christianity is worth exploring further. To help you there, I have listed some information regarding my books on Christianity. But the focus of this book is, quite simply, marriage.

Let me say something here about the tone of this book. Ideally, the best scenario for dealing with marriage issues would be for us to talk together about them in a cosy and private one-to-one conversation over a coffee, a beer or a glass of wine. Because this book is a substitute for that, what I have tried to do is keep a friendly and open conversational tone. So, although this book was written in collaboration with Dr Chris Walley, we realised at a very early stage that it would be most effective if we used 'I' and 'my', rather than the more distant and impersonal 'we' and 'our' throughout the book. Chris has been married to Alison for 23 years and they have two teenage sons, John and Mark. Let me add another comment here. Although Chris and I have tried to make this a lively and relevant book rather than a formal treatise on marriage, we have deliberately avoided bringing in personal anecdotes drawn from our marriages. This is partly to protect the innocent (and the guilty!) but also because we wanted to look at general principles rather than personalities. But to compensate for the lack of personal illustrations, there is a brief story at the start of each chapter that sets the scene and raises some of the issues. The people in these, and other illustrations, are purely fictional creations.

Four Aims

I have had four aims in this book: humility, honesty, helpfulness and hope. Let me deal with each of these in turn.

Humility

I suppose you could, in theory, write an arrogant book on marriage. You could tell people exactly how their relationship ought to work, because this is the way that you have done it. Not only is this *not* that sort of book, but I don't see how any sane person could ever be arrogant about marriage. Marriage (like having children) tends to undermine pride. Although I take delight in having been happily married for 21 years to Killy, I am not inclined to boast about it. The credit for that goes elsewhere. When I see a failed marriage, my reaction is simply and genuinely this: there but for the grace of God go Killy and I. Of course, humility is not the same as saying that you don't have any answers. I believe there are answers (why would I write this book if I didn't believe that?) and I have done my best to write them down in this book.

I have also tried to avoid giving the impression that only Christians have good marriages. There are splendid marriages between those who are not Christians and there are some bad Christian marriages. But many Christians would freely admit that, if they and their spouse had not had a real faith in Christ, their marriage would not have survived.

I also want to say that this is not a confrontational book and that I have not set out to accuse or to inflict injury. After all, far too many people have already acquired enough wounds in this area and I have no desire to add to them. One group of people I want to particularly address, and it is an increasingly large one, are those whose experience of marriage is such that – perhaps embittered, guilty and confused – they have turned their backs on it. I not only believe in marriage, I also believe (and for the same reasons) in forgiveness and healing.

Mind you, don't confuse the desire to be gentle with a wish to be bland and harmless. There are, for instance, some myths about marriage in our society that are so harmful that I cannot, in all honesty, be gentle about them. Some of these beliefs have done so much damage that I can only treat them in the harshest way.

And while we are on the subject of humility, I ought to confess that, as I look at this manuscript, I realise that there is little here that is truly new. I doubt that I have come up with any innovative tricks for marriage, made any new discoveries into the human psyche or had any radical insights into male-female relationships. What I have aimed to do is compile, refine and update the wisdom and advice that has kept marriages together through the most difficult circumstances imaginable for thousands of years and express it in a new way. This is a book not of discovery, but of rediscovery. Actually, I suspect that for many people this wisdom is so unfamiliar that it will come over as strangely novel.

Honesty

Another aim that I have sought in writing this book is honesty. I want to say that this book offers no easy solutions. I would love to claim that within these pages could be found six instant ways to improve your marriage and that within a week you could enjoy the marriage of your dreams. It isn't that simple. A human being is a complex and fallible creature, capable of doing illogical, stupid and wrong things, and marriage is two such creatures trying (and often not succeeding) to live together. Precisely because it is so complex, creating a good marriage is not like assembling Ikea furniture or even baking a cake – there are no step-by-step solutions and no recipes.

Helpfulness

A third aim is to be helpful. The whole point of writing this book is not to score points or 'defend the traditional Christian position' – it is, above all, to help. This book is not a meditation on the mystery and beauty of marriage or one of those little inspirational books along the lines of 'A Dozen Happy Thoughts to Lighten Dark Days'. This book has been written as a practical support and encouragement to those who are married. I want to be like a doctor – where there is a healthy marriage, I want to help it stay that way and where there is a sick marriage, I want to do what I can to bring healing.

Hope

A final aim of this book is to hold out hope. After all, there is no shortage of cynicism about marriage. In fact, in researching this book, I have realised that I could easily compile an entirely different book: *The Anthology of Vicious Quotes on Marriage*. It would include such sayings as Oscar Wilde's 'Bigamy is having one wife too many. Monogamy is the same', Cher's 'The problem with most women is that they get all excited about nothing and then marry him' and the anonymous 'If it weren't for marriage, men and women would have to fight with total strangers'. Funny as they may be (and there are many, many more of them), my attitude here is different. Quite simply, I believe in marriage. I believe in it in the sense that I have faith, that it is something for which the human race is designed. But I also believe in it in the sense that I know that it can be something wonderful and splendid. Yes, I have seen marriages that resembled war zones but I have also seen marriages that were outstanding successes and were places of great healing and blessing. As you start this book I want you to know that, for all the difficulties, I believe that poor marriages can be made to work well and good marriages can be made to work even better.

About this Book

Throughout the book I have inserted quotes that have struck me as appropriate, or witty or both. Whether I agree with them or not, I will leave you to guess! While every effort has been made to trace and acknowledge the sources of all the quotes, I want to apologise for any omissions or misquotation. Quotes cited without an author are believed to be anonymous.

I have deliberately kept Bible references and quotations to a minimum. If you want to follow them up, do use a modern translation of the Bible. I'd recommend either the New International Version (NIV) or the New Living Translation (NLT) – a version that I think is especially good at communicating the meaning of the passage. Where I have quoted here from the Bible, I have used the NLT.

The layout of the book is as follows. There are TWO parts and EIGHT chapters. Part ONE (Chapters 1–3) looks at the building of a marriage and covers the principles and practice of married life. Part TWO (Chapters 4–7) centres on defending marriage and looks at resolving conflicts, affair-proofing, and achieving an enduring marriage. A final brief 'Perspective' chapter brings together some of the themes of the book.

PART ONE

Building a Marriage

Chapter 1

The Practice of Marriage (1)
Twelve Basic Principles

By nine o'clock Gwen was only half way through writing her end of year reports and feeling increasingly irritated by the fact that she had not heard from Nathan. 'I didn't get married to spend my evenings alone in an empty house', she muttered under her breath.

A few minutes later, Nathan called. 'Hi Gwen, it's me.' The tone was apologetic and in the background she could hear talking and music. 'Look love, we've been working late and I thought I'd join the lads for a quick pint.'

'I see,' Gwen said, realising as she spoke that she was using the same tone she used with her more difficult pupils. 'So when can I expect you back?'

'Well . . .' There was a pause. 'Don't wait up for me!

'As if!' she retorted.

'Sorry love,' Nathan said, 'but you have all that marking to do.'

'Reports!' she replied, more sharply than she meant. 'I told you last night.'

'Whatever. See you later.'

Fuming, Gwen put the pile of reports to one side and opened a new document on the computer. Quickly she typed the heading 'End of Year Report on Nathan' and then, suddenly, she found that she was typing almost without thinking, the words angrily punching themselves onto the screen.

This is a disappointing report. In his first year of marriage, Nathan has consistently failed to live up to his promise. Socially, his attitude to marriage can be summed up by his 'hilarious' joke that brides wear white at weddings so they can match other kitchen appliances. He has yet to learn that my tastes in videos extend beyond the categories of Action, Adventure and Horror. He still fails to realise that my idea of a good night out is not four pints in a smoky and noisy bar listening to stupid blokes tell bad jokes.

In Domestic Science he has proved to be an under-achiever. After a year, he still fails to appreciate that fresh toilet rolls do not instantly materialise from nowhere. He seems to consider that grime and household dust are either harmless natural occurrences or optical illusions that are visible only to women. As far as clothes go, he still believes that there is a category of 'Filthy but Wearable'. He has yet to appreciate that rubbish needs taking out.

In the area of Communication Skills, Nathan's ability has, if anything, declined. It has become apparent that, far from representing attempts to communicate, such expressions as 'Uh huh', 'Yes love', 'Right', 'That's interesting dear' and 'Whatever' are merely verbal noises and simply mean 'Don't distract me. I'm thinking of something else.'

In terms of Physical Fitness, Nathan has put on 12 pounds in the first year of marriage. On this basis, we will have to strengthen the floors within a decade.

Psychologically, it has become apparent that Nathan laments the fact that it is no longer acceptable to gather 30 friends, put on horned helmets, get roaring drunk and go and pillage a nearby town.

Achievements: He has learned to change his socks and underwear daily.

Conclusion: Were it possible, I would send Nathan for retraining at a remedial institution.

Gwen sat back and stared at her handiwork. If it wasn't about my husband, she thought sadly, it would be very funny. But what do I do about it?

Introduction

This is the first of six chapters on building and defending a marriage. In this chapter, I want to look at the principles of being married, and in the following two chapters the bonds of marriage in the sexual (Chapter 2), social, psychological, and spiritual areas (Chapter 3). In these chapters I have deliberately placed the emphasis on the positive side of marriage and talked mainly about enhancing the wellbeing of a marriage. In Chapters 4–6, our attention switches to the problems that can occur in marriage and deals with conflict resolution and affair-proofing. This division into positive and negative chapters is deliberate. Surrounded as we are by failed or failing marriages, it is all too easy to see a marriage as being little more than two people engaged in a lifelong process of disaster preven-

> *There is no more lovely, friendly and charming relationship, communion or company than a good marriage.*
>
> **Martin Luther**

tion. While recognising that difficulties do exist in marriages, I want these first three chapters to be affirming. Of course, there are links between affirming marriage and defending it: as with medicine, prevention is easier than cure and the 'sicknesses' and 'diseases' of marriage are much less easy to catch if your relationship is in good health. Nevertheless, as you read these chapters I want you to feel positive and encouraged about marriage!

Specifically in this chapter, I want to bring together a number of ideas on enhancing marriage and try to summarise them in 12 basic principles. But don't think of these principles as being separate from each other: see them, rather, as interlocking and overlapping skills. You cannot isolate principles like 'showing love' or 'making an effort' from 'communicating' or 'admitting your mistakes'.

1. Remember That You Need to Make an Effort at Marriage

Physicists tell us that one of the key laws of the universe is that, over time, things tend to become disorganised and chaotic. Actually, anyone who has seen a teenager's bedroom may wonder why we need physicists to tell us this. But the general principle has a far wider application: left to themselves, things do tend to fall apart. You could call it the 'Principle of the Built-in Negative Tendency' and as a principle, it applies to marriages as much as to anything else. It is important to recognise that there is a negative spiritual and psychological force that, unless constantly opposed, will drag a marriage down. Behind this 'Built-in Negative Tendency' in human affairs, Christians would see the reality of what the Bible calls 'sin': the results of us – and our world – being in rebellion against God. From the point of view of looking after your marriage, whether or not you accept that as an explanation makes very little practical difference. The fact is that unless effort is put into it, problems will automatically occur in a marriage.

One of the difficulties here is that sometimes we find this negative tendency hard to believe. For instance, during a honeymoon or in the course of a romantic evening out, it is easy to think that your marriage is like a balloon, capable of resisting gravity and staying aloft effortlessly for ever. And if you let Hollywood or the media guide your thinking, then this is the myth that is presented to you on an almost daily basis: a marriage is an effortless and lighter than air phenomenon – just relax and enjoy! The reality, though, is that a marriage is not a balloon, it is a plane, and it requires power (and skill) to stop it from crashing into the ground.

Even when a marriage is made in heaven the maintenance work has to be done on earth.

A fundamental principle of any successful marriage is that an input of effort is required. It is incredibly naive to think that any successful marriage – an intimate, long-term relationship between two people – can be achieved without the investment of work and time. There is another danger here: that if you believe that marriage should be easy, and you find that it is not, then you might think that something is wrong. The reality is that all marriages need maintenance. There are four aspects of love: craving, companionship, caring and commitment love. Each, in its own way, requires hard work. Frankly, many people are more willing to work hard at the success of their careers than at the success of their marriages.

Certainly, the Bible is under no illusion that marriage is a smooth sail on calm waters with a gentle wind behind you. In the letter to the Ephesians, Paul says the following: 'And you husbands must love your wives with the same love Christ showed the church. He gave up his life for her' (Eph. 5:25). The command here is to love, not just as long as things are going well, but even when it is so hard that your life is on the line. A love that is not prepared to be sacrificial is not love in the Bible's sense of the word.

The work in marriage may be physical. For instance, it may involve doing extra chores to help your spouse. But it may be work in other ways: perhaps spending time listening to them, giving up your favourite TV programme to help them on some project, or bowing to their wishes in some other manner. Now of course, a marriage is not all hard work. It is rather like cross-country cycling: there are glorious downhill stretches where you can freewheel, but either side of those are the parts where you have to do some stiff pedalling, and sometimes there is no option but to get off and push.

It is easy to imagine that a marriage is a partnership where husband and wife each contribute 50 per cent, but it is not. In reality, it is a merger where each side contributes 100 per cent and sometimes it may seem like more. But without the expenditure of effort, a marriage will go nowhere – instead, it will fall apart.

2. Make the Success of Your Marriage Your Main Priority

In our modern world, a vast number of things clamour for our attention. We have to keep our jobs, pay our mortgages or rent, work on the house, meet our friends, keep fit, walk the dog, do the garden and so on. To make your marriage your main priority means to resolve, in the face of all these demands (and others), to put your marriage first so that nothing else gets in the way.

I can imagine two objections to this. The first might be from someone who says that this is an impossible demand because their career depends on their total commitment to work. Yet, even on practical terms, that objection could be challenged. After all, while a successful marriage can be an enormous help to a career, a failed marriage (with all its psychological hurts, stresses and negative financial repercussions) can be devastating. And to treat the welfare of your spouse as secondary to your job is actually to undermine the whole basis of marriage. The second objection might be from a Christian saying that, surely, God comes first. Of course, that is right, but in reality I can think of very few situations indeed where God's commands would go against the overall good of a marriage. Yes, you do hear of people having such an intense and busy ministry for God that their own marriage suffers, but I am dubious whether this pleases God. Far too often, the cause is that the person concerned is a workaholic (and there are no workaholics as bad as those who think that they are working for God) who has simply failed to establish priorities. Actually, in an age such as ours where marriage is under threat, I think a major task of all Christians (whether they are in full-time service or not) is to show the reality of their faith by their marriages. A happy and successful Christian marriage, especially one that has survived difficult circumstances, can say more about the reality of how Jesus changes lives than a lot of sermons. If you believe that God called you to get married, then your task is to stay married.

Let me make five practical suggestions here:

a) Bring your marriage into your decision-making

In making decisions on anything other than trivial matters have a rule to always ask yourself what the effect of your choices will be on your marriage. Will the results be for good or bad? On the same basis, evaluate everything else you do, such as going out with your friends or your hobbies and sports, on the basis of whether they impact negatively or positively on your marriage.

b) *Take positive action to keep your marriage as your main priority*

Make spending time with your spouse a main concern. If you are both busy people, then make appointments together in your diaries well in advance and consider them as virtually unbreakable. It may sound strange to make appointments with your spouse, but sometimes it is necessary. Equally, you might want to identify the main challenge to a marriage as being your number one priority and make a stand in that area. For instance, if it is your work that is intruding into your time together then you might want to indicate gently to your boss where your priorities lie. Sometimes that can be done positively, so, for instance, when you are asked to work on a Saturday when you have a long-planned day out together with your spouse, you might offer to work late on a Friday instead. Sometimes you may just have to make your position plain. But if those around you know that your marriage is your main priority, then there is less chance (but no guarantee) that they will accidentally put pressure on you in a way that will be harmful to it.

c) *Seek to handle pressures so that they bind you together rather than push you apart*

All marriages have pressures put on them (work demands, ill health, shortages of money, etc.), and sometimes the impact of these forces can be severe. Such pressures can be handled in two ways. The bad way is to let the forces generated come between you and your spouse; the good way is to let them push you closer. So, for instance, if a man has a problem in his work, he can let his tension explode in the evenings towards his wife with harmful consequences for the marriage. On the other hand, if both he and his wife have made their marriage their priority, then they may be able to view these work problems as pressures that are directed against them as a couple. So he may say to her 'I think we have a problem' and ask her advice. In building an arch,

An important ingredient in a marriage is to treat all disasters as incidents and none of the incidents as disasters.

it is constructed so that when the force of gravity pushes down on it the structure is held tighter together. A marriage should be like this, so that when pressure comes upon it, the sole effect of the pressure should be that of strengthening the marriage.

d) Celebrate your achievements in marriage

We live in a culture in which we are encouraged to live for the moment and which has little time for the past. Yet, forgetting the past can be dangerous, and in marriage, remembering is a definite virtue. What you have achieved so far in marriage should be an encouragement for you to maintain it as your priority. It's a bit like running a long race: the memory of having already completed so many laps is an encouragement to continue. So maintain photo albums, scrapbooks, keepsakes, and have times of remembering and revisiting places; keep anniversaries, celebrate marriage landmarks and be grateful. Once a marriage loses its past, then its future is threatened. Of course, Christians would want to include God in their thankfulness.

Incidentally, those of us outside a marriage should do all we can to help in honouring such achievements. In some ways, wedding anniversaries are more worthy of celebration than birthdays. After all, to get a birthday, you merely have to survive, but to get a wedding anniversary you have to achieve something. In these days that are so difficult for marriage, we should, perhaps, view our friend's wedding anniversaries as pilots viewed their colleagues returning from bombing missions in the Second World War – with a celebration of survival against hostile fire.

e) Don't allow for the possibility of failure

Another good rule is to make the success of your marriage such a personal priority that you do not consider the prospect of failure a possibility. Agree between you (and there is no better time than before marriage) that neither divorce nor an affair is an option. Now by doing this, you are not simply engaging in wishful thinking and refusing to face up to reality, what you are doing is making a statement of your determination to succeed or die trying. There is good psychology here: in any conflict, those with one eye on the exit usually lose out. In 1519, Hernando Cortéz landed his fleet of eleven ships on the eastern coast of Mexico with the intention of defeating the Aztec Empire. He was so determined to be victorious that he gave the order that all the boats should be burnt to make retreat impossible. A similar commitment to success and a refusal to allow the possibility of failure is vital in a marriage. Agree that the only way forward is together.

3. Take the Initiative

Because of the way human nature is, the temptation is always to react to events after they happen, rather than to seize the initiative beforehand. Such a strategy can, however, be bad news, because it is all too easy to slide into a situation where you are in permanent crisis management mode. It is far better to be proactive than retroactive in marriage, and to take action sooner rather than later. By taking the initiative, you are also fighting against the all too common trend of drifting. Drifting is bad for several reasons: if you drift, it is all too easy to find yourself either going nowhere (bad) or heading onto the rocks (worse). To take the initiative is to choose to act first rather than react later.

Being proactive or taking the initiative has two aspects, negative and positive. Negatively, to take the initiative is to look for hazards ahead and to plan for them. After all, some things in life can be foreseen. So, for example, you can predict with some accuracy the effect of a baby's arrival in a family: the loss of earnings, the increased costs, the changed social routine and so on. Equally, the effects of retirement are well known and can be planned for, both financially and psychologically. To take the initiative here is to spend time together thinking about such things and making sure, as far as you can, that you are prepared for them. So if you are both heading into new and busy jobs, taking the initiative might involve sitting down together and deliberately scheduling into your diaries evenings together. In the teaching of Advanced Driving techniques, a key skill is to 'read the road ahead' and to anticipate danger long before it happens. All marriages need a similar ability.

The positive aspect of taking the initiative is more subtle: it is to have a purpose and a direction to your marriage and to set yourself goals. It is to ask yourselves as a couple what you want your marriage to do and to be. Do you want to 'just survive' as a couple or do you want to have a marriage that you can be proud of? Do you have wider goals? Perhaps of helping others, or doing something for your community? I realise that even to suggest such things these days is to risk ridicule, but surely there is more to a marriage than a couple (plus or minus a few children) snuggled up cosily together behind locked doors? To say 'I want to leave the world a better place' may be a cliché but it is still a valuable statement. Here, as elsewhere, there is a Christian distinctive. The Christian couple ought to be able to say that they do have a purpose: that they want to serve God. But Christian or not, it is always worth any married couple asking each other what the purpose of their marriage is. If your marriage had a mission statement, what would it be?

Incidentally, let me offer a word of warning here. It is essential that both partners in a marriage agree on taking the initiative and how to take it. One party in a marriage having a vision and deciding to follow it alone, is guaranteed to generate stress.

4. Communicate!

Communication is of vital importance in marriage. Communication is the blood supply of any relationship: damage it and the relationship starts to die.

Guidelines on communication are: communicate at a deep level, be aware of body language, learn to understand your spouse's language and be aware of the risks of miscommunication. I want to talk about two important attitudes that need to be learned: on the one hand, to work to develop better communication skills and, on the other, to protect good communication skills by working to avoid existing skills being damaged.

Develop Good Communication Skills

The first thing you need is to seek, constantly, to communicate more effectively. Despite the existence of many studies on how people communicate with each other, good communication seems to be a threatened ability these days. For all the volume and quantity of words expressed today, there seems to be a real shortage of good, deep and meaningful communication

The first duty of Love is to listen.

Paul Tillich

in marriage. I suspect that television must take something of the blame with its regular intrusion into a married life: it is surely more than symbolic that when a couple watch TV they face the screen and not each other. All too frequently, the family circle turns into a semicircle.

Let me make some suggestions of how to improve communication in a marriage.

- Make good and effective communication a priority. Remember that the automatic ability to mind read does not come free with every wedding ring. Be committed to helping each other learn the skill of effective communication.
- Make it a rule to spend more time in conversation. This may mean making suitable opportunities for conversation. For example, eat meals together, ban the TV and the radio from the eating area, and have a 'no reading at the table' rule. You may even want to let the answerphone take any calls. Try to have some time every day when you and your spouse can talk about things without being interrupted by anybody. Even discussion about trivial things can be important. Try to increase the time you spend talking with your spouse. It may even be that what you need to do right now is to put this book down (temporarily!) and go and spend some time talking with them.
- Be courteous and tender. Conversation should be a

delicate and sensitive dialogue, not hitting each other over the head with blunt words. Remember, in a marriage you are not in the business of scoring verbal points over each other. In speaking, always try low volume first. And remember that nothing discourages conversation as much as a harsh response does.

If you are patient in one moment of anger, you will escape a hundred days of sorrow.

Chinese Proverb

- Learn to express yourself effectively. Men, in particular, often need to work at expressing their feelings in a meaningful way.
- Learn to listen. Be responsive to one another and practice listening with your mouth shut. In other words, don't interrupt your spouse until you have heard all that they have to say. Give them time to make themselves clearly understood and make sure that what you understood them to say was, in fact, what they really meant.
- Be supportive! Validate and encourage your spouse in your conversation. In your conversation, don't kick your spouse when they are down. If your spouse dents the car, he or she doesn't want to come home to an angry response. They want support and a shoulder to cry on.

The real art of conversation is not only to say the right thing in the right place, but to leave unsaid the wrong thing at the tempting moment.

Dorothy Nevell

- We all know that some of the most important moments in a marriage may be when a couple are in bed together. Yet, the marriage bed is important, not just because it is the place of sexual intimacy, but because it is also the place of psychological intimacy. Those discussions in the dark just before falling asleep may be the most critical ones in a marriage. So try to stay awake for them!

- Yes, work at communication but, at the same time, respect your spouse's privacy and need for space. Frankly, this is a difficult balance to strike. A husband or wife should have 'room to breathe' and be able to go and do something on their own. Some marriages need that sort of space.

Protect Good Communication Skills

It is not enough just to create good communication skills, they need to be maintained so that your good ability to communicate does not weaken with time. The 'Principle of the Built-in Negative Tendency' that I described earlier is never more damaging than here. Let me summarise four specific threats to communication that can appear in the course of a marriage.

Threat 1: The plateau effect

People who study the learning of language point out that people often fail to go on to fully learn a language because they reach a plateau and stop there. The language plateau is a level of knowledge where you can get by adequately and so feel that there is no need to work at going any further. A similar problem faces married couples trying to understand each other. They learn enough to communicate about the basics (what to eat, where to go, how to spend money) but don't bother trying to go beyond that, so they fail to

> *The heart of marriage is its communication system. It can be said that the success and happiness of any married pair is measurable in terms of the deepening dialogue which characterises their union.*
>
> **Dwight Small**

acquire the skills to enable them to talk about how they feel at the very deepest of levels. The only way round this is to encourage each other beyond the plateau. Make a point of trying to discuss things at a deep level and of expressing how you feel about things that have strongly affected you. So, if your spouse says of some film you watched, 'I thought it was great', don't just let them get away with that. Ask them why they thought it was great. Learn to communicate better.

Threat 2: Creeping silences

In a marriage, another problem can occur over time: that, slowly, like weeds in a garden, silences creep in. Nothing is said, because it seems that there is nothing to say. The routine of life has become so regular that words are, apparently, not needed. Of course, marriages do not have to be a non-stop babbling brook of talk, but the danger with the creeping silences is that the ability to share thoughts erodes away. This is something that needs to be overcome. Encourage discussion between you, inject stimulus into your life, get hobbies, switch the TV off, and above all, talk to each other. Why is it that you can spot the married couples in a restaurant because they are the only couples who aren't talking to each other?

Threat 3: Unexploded bombs

In some cases, what happens is that there is a row over a particular issue and harsh and hurtful words are exchanged. The row is never settled and, as a result, unexploded bombs remain scattered around the topic that was at the heart of the row. So, for instance, a couple has a dispute over whether or not he should change his job. It is never resolved so, as a coping mechanism, they refuse to talk about it (or anything close to it) lest they cause further explosions. The result is that a major issue has now become 'off limits'. After a few more such incidents, whole areas of life can become sealed off as 'no-go' areas where you just don't talk. And, as many of the areas are vital ones (which is why you fought so hard over them in the first place) you have a serious problem. The solution to this is twofold. First, early on in marriage, develop 'rules of engagement' that will enable you to handle issues without hurting each other. It may be that you decide not to say things that are hurtful and make rules about what can be said. Second, you learn to practice forgiveness in order to try to defuse the issues and make them harmless. This is something that I will talk more about in Chapter 4.

> *Love is not blind – it sees more and not less, but because it sees more it is willing to see less.*

Threat 4: Increasing deafness

Later on in a marriage, physical deafness may cause communication problems. But far more serious (and capable of starting much earlier) is a psychological or behavioural deafness where one (or both) of the people in marriage ceases to listen to what the other is saying. It is probably most commonly caused by boredom. Endlessly caricatured in comedies – 'Yes, dear,' 'Whatever you say, dear,' 'Absolutely, dear' – it can be a serious disease of a marriage and a major threat to effective communication. Make an effort to listen.

5. Make Time for Marriage

For a marriage to thrive you need to make space and time for it. Have time for each other, and if you haven't time, then make it. Incidentally, this is particularly important after children enter the marriage. If your spouse needs to talk to you, then I can think of very few legitimate excuses (stopping a bleeding artery, perhaps) for not immediately listening.

If both of you have busy lives, then it is worth specifically scheduling time together so that, for instance, both of you know that Tuesday nights are off limits for meetings or anything else that might come up. Some people suggest that, for the wisest use of time, you should distinguish three types of meeting: *Dating Nights, Planning Times* and *Problem Management Sessions*. Let me explain the distinction and why it is worth making it.

Dating Nights are fun nights. Remember those nights out before you were married? Well, nowhere in any wedding service that I have heard of does it say that 'they must cease forthwith'. Continue dating: go out, have a meal, take a walk, see a movie together. If you can, extend it over a weekend or longer and stretch a dating night into a dating week. These times should be (as far as it is in your power) purely for pleasure. If you think of your marriage as being like a financial account, then dating nights are like putting money into the account. They strengthen your relationship as husband and wife, and when you come (as you will) to have tough times, then these will be there as a support.

Planning Sessions are different. These are, effectively, the business meetings of marriages, where you find somewhere quiet to sit down and discuss at leisure how things are going. The brief of these meetings is just to review matters and to make plans for the future. So you might bring maps and brochures and think about your holidays, or talk about what you ought to do on the house next. Planning sessions are marriage business times, but they still ought to be laid-back and relaxing.

Problem Management Sessions are, as their name

suggests, meetings where you have a specific issue or problem to deal with. So, when the finances are in a mess, it's time to have a Problem Management Session. Set a time and find a suitable place and try to tackle the specific issue. Unfortunately, it is in the nature of things that these can be tense meetings, fraught with the potential for rows and recriminations. But every marriage needs, once in a while, to set aside time to deal with specific problems. Although it is tempting to leave problems alone, neglecting issues rarely results in them going away, they just pop up again later – only the second time around they are a lot harder to deal with.

Now when you think about these three types of meeting, do you see why they need to be kept separate? Imagine looking forward to a gentle, relaxing and romantic evening out, only to have it turn into a dull planning session on the fate of the garden or, even worse, a tense and strained problem management session on how to pay the mortgage?

Parkinson's Law says that 'work expands to fill the time available for its completion'. The same principle applies to a marriage. In theory, most married couples have a vast amount of time to share with each other. In practice, unless you take deliberate action, trivial matters will creep in and fill up that time.

6. Think Long Term

One of the characteristics of our society today is the emphasis on instant results and a reluctance to think long term. Our ancestors built cathedrals, palaces and monuments expecting them to last for centuries. In contrast, we throw up shopping malls and theme parks knowing (and hardly caring) that they will be torn down in, at the most, a few decades. After all, who cares or wants to think about tomorrow? 'I want it and I want it now!' and 'Why wait for tomorrow, when you can get it today?' are slogans of an age whose defining symbol might as well be the microwave. This general mood, like so many others, filters through into our marriages. Couples expect instant results and instant gratification and they get fed up when neither are forthcoming. The inevitable result is increased stress. He may expect stunning sex from day one of the marriage; she may expect perfect understanding before the wedding presents have been opened.

In contrast, I believe that it is vital for a marriage to be seen as a long-term project and not as a series of 'give-it-me-now experiences'. Of course, to do this only makes sense if (as I am assuming) you have made marriage a permanent lifetime commitment. After all, if you think of your marriage as a short-term event (the relationship equivalent of disposable cutlery), then to think in terms of years makes little sense.

To hold to this long-term view brings two implications. The first is the idea that you shouldn't be disappointed if something, whether it is sex or your social life, doesn't deliver wonders overnight. The second is that it is an encouragement to act with long-term plans in view. Think of someone whose financial investments mature, giving them a good pay-out. They can either reap the dividend and spend it, or they can reinvest to ensure long-term profits in the future. In marriage, you are in the business of long-term investment. So the time spent working at a marriage in the early days may have a pay-off after many years.

> *Advice to Men – The best thing you can do for your children is to love their mother.*
>
> **Anon**

Again, there is a Christian perspective here. Unlike so many people, Christians have a positive view of the future. Tomorrow doesn't scare us and we don't need instant gratification for the present. We, of all people, can afford to wait. Whether you share that Christian perspective or not, you need to be prepared to do things that will take time. Pace your marriage.

7. Learn to Understand Each Other

The idea that men and women are very different in terms of their behaviour is something that numerous books are now proclaiming as an astonishing revelation. I suspect that it is a truth which most wise husbands and wives have always known, but that they probably just took for granted.

Hundreds of behavioural differences between men and women have been listed, some are fundamental, some are mysterious, and some are just downright trivial. Let me list just a few of my own favourites:

- Most women have left adolescence permanently by the time they are eighteen. Men stay in the adolescent state until they are at least thirty, and then leave it only temporarily – under the influence of alcohol, adolescence returns.
- Men are single-tasking, and can do one thing well at a time. Women are multi-tasking: they can do many different things at once. In the time that it takes a man in his single-tasking way to drink a cup of coffee and have a slice of toast, a woman can eat breakfast, make the children's sandwiches, write a shopping list, counsel a sobbing child, make a phone call and feed the cat.
- Men and women have very different attitudes to

marriage. A woman marries a man expecting that he will change (but he doesn't), while a man marries a woman expecting that she won't change (but she does). Most wives think that their husbands got a prize when they married them; most husbands think they should have been given a reward instead.

- Women grow out of playing with toys; men never do. As they grow older their toys simply become more expensive and more complex. They also have thicker instruction manuals: something that is a total waste of time as men rarely read them anyway.

- A woman cannot imagine good sex without romance. A man thinks they are two different things.

- Men are never lost, especially in the presence of women. They intuitively know the right way. Any failure to get to where they want to go to is always because the signs have been moved, the planners have renamed the streets, or their wives gave them the wrong directions.

- Even in a state of inebriation men have no difficulty in undressing a woman in pitch darkness. However, even when sober and in broad daylight, they are incapable of fitting a small child into a Babygro.

- When there is a problem with a car, a man will open the bonnet, stare at the engine as if he knows what he is doing and mutter magic words like *carburettor*, *timing belt* and *distributor leads*. He does this despite the fact that a) he hasn't the slightest clue what any of them are and b) his car almost certainly isn't fitted with them anyway. Eventually, he calls for help, something that a woman would have done an hour earlier.

- A woman spends an hour making a list of things she needs and then goes to the supermarket and spends 45 minutes buying them. A man waits till the only items left in his fridge are a half-empty jar of mayonnaise and a mouldy tomato. He then goes shopping and spends two hours buying everything that looks good.

- A woman knows all about her children: their teachers, their dental appointments, their best friends, their secret fears and dreams. A man is vaguely aware of some short people living in the house.
- Men wear one pair of shoes all day; women like to change theirs at least three times.
- Men see the telephone as a communications tool and use it to send short vital messages to other people. Women use the telephone as a means of social bonding and, after seeing someone for two hours for lunch, are still capable of calling them that evening to talk for another hour.
- Men imagine that they are so tough they can handle a compound fracture as if it was a minor scratch. The reality is that when they catch a cold they lie in bed moaning and need someone to bring them soup. Women keep going.
- A woman believes that visitors will be impressed by a clean house. A man believes that visitors will be impressed with his large hi-fi, computer or TV set-up.
- A man has to hold the television remote control while he watches TV and to constantly change channels. If a remote has been misplaced, psychological trauma is inevitable until it is found.
- In today's liberated age, men and women now share the housework. The woman does the laundry, the cooking, the cleaning and the dishes. The man does the rest.

Now of course, these illustrations are, to some extent, tongue-in-cheek and exaggerated. Nevertheless, it is surprising how much truth there is in them. Men and women are indeed very different. They may not speak a totally different language, but it is almost certainly a different dialect.

But what are the implications of recognising these differences for a marriage? Well, it destroys the myth that men and women are sufficiently alike that if a husband or wife wants to know what their spouse wants, they need only ask what they themselves would want under such circumstances. This old myth[1] has come to be replaced by a new one: that men and women are so fundamentally different that they are effectively aliens to each other. The implications of this view are that the best you can hope for between men and women is a limited, strained and flawed understanding of each other. This view can be (and is) used to justify marriage breakdown: 'After all,' the argument goes, 'we could never really understand each other.'

The reality is, I believe, something different. Men and women are indeed different, but in a complementary way. Psychologically, they match each other in the way that a key fits a lock or a plug fits a socket. The way in which men and women can physically interconnect in sexual intercourse is a visible image of how they can interlock mentally and psychologically. There are gender differences, but those differences need not be barriers. Nevertheless, the fact remains that you should never assume that your spouse sees things the way you do or that their problems can be solved in the way that you would solve them.

Several specific differences are worth highlighting. Men and women have different needs in a marriage.

---

[1] Actually, the idea that anybody ever held such a view beyond the first few days of a honeymoon may itself be a myth.

Most women seem to want, above all, affection, conversation, openness, security and commitment. In contrast, men would put sexual fulfilment, companionship, physical attractiveness, good looks, domestic support and admiration at the top of their need list in a marriage. So, for instance, a woman might be happy to marry a man who was plain, but who fulfilled her other needs. A man is much less likely to marry on the same basis. Certainly too, women are more emotion-centred and that side of a relationship is critical to them. For better or worse, men can live with an emotionally low-temperature relationship as long as everything else is okay.

However, it is dangerous to generalise and say that 'all women are like this' and 'all men are like that'. Not only are there differences between the sexes, but there are differences within them too. Everyone is different. The best suggestion is to assume that your spouse does, in fact, see things differently to you and to look out for those differences. Ask them how they react and feel towards issues or events. And when they come up with some opinion that astounds you, don't consider them defective or stupid because they see things a different way. They may repay the compliment!

> *Husband's admission: 'All right, you don't understand me. I don't suppose Mrs Einstein understood Albert either.'*

8. Think of Your Marriage as a Team

In a society whose emphasis is towards individualism ('you do your thing and I'll do mine'), it is easy for people to see a marriage as just two individuals who have no greater bond than that they have both agreed to go (more or less) in the same direction. Yet, a marriage is more than

this: there is a sense in which there is a genuine and deep
unity between the man and the wife. In a marriage where
this unity is real, it is often shown by language used: the
talk is of 'we' rather than 'you and me' and 'us' rather
than 'she and I' or 'he and I'.

This unity is something that needs to be encouraged
and one way of doing this is to think of your marriage
relationship as a team. It is essential that, as husband and
wife, you do not see yourselves as two individuals who
currently share the same bed, surname and postal
address. You must recognise that you are a team with
shared mutual concerns and an interlocked future.
Consider that what hurts your spouse hurts you and
what is good for them is good for you. Your priority is
that you put the team interests first and your own
second. We have all heard of talented people who have
been dropped from some sports or business organisation
because they are not 'team players'. In a marriage, both
parties need to remember
that the good of the mar-
riage comes before the
good of the individuals
that make up that mar-
riage.

*To be happy with a man you
must understand him a lot
and love him a little. To be
happy with a woman you
must love her a lot and not
try to understand her at all.*

One practical expression
of this teamwork can be seen in the way that many
successful marriages have a division of responsibility
within them. Whether consciously or not, they end up
acting rather like governments, so that responsibility for
the various components of a household (the finances, the
children's education, running the home, keeping the car
going, supervising the garden maintenance and so on)
are shared between them. At its best, this policy works
wonderfully well, although, as I will point out in the next
chapter, there can be problems. Nevertheless, it is a good

idea to think of your marriage as two people who are *inter*dependent rather than *in*dependent.

9. Admit Your Mistakes and Forgive Theirs

In every marriage, mistakes are made and wrong things are done. These issues may be as trivial as forgetting to post a letter for your spouse or as serious as admitting an affair. As everybody from the age of two upwards knows, there are three possible responses when we make a mistake or do something wrong: we can try to hide it, we can blame someone else for it or we can admit we did it. The first response is unhelpful in a marriage, and the second, especially where we blame our spouse, is positively harmful. But although the third response, that of admission of guilt (I would use 'confession' but it sounds too religious) is the right one, it is also a response that is hard to make. To admit guilt is to open yourself up to rebuke (or punishment) and it diminishes your authority. Yet, without an admission of guilt, there can be no real possibility of resolving matters. Remember the story at the start of this chapter. It is hard to see any other way for things to be patched up between Gwen and Nathan, without Nathan a) recognising that he is not being as fully committed to the marriage as he should be and b) genuinely apologising for his attitude.

A good marriage is the union of two forgivers.

The reality is that people are only likely to voluntarily admit guilt where there is the likelihood of forgiveness. The dynamics of a marriage are strongly affected by whether or not the possibility of forgiveness exists within it. Where forgiveness only occurs grudgingly (or not at all), you can end up with a sort of point-scoring relationship, where both sides are permanently on their guard against each other. In contrast, where there is an atmosphere of forgiveness and acceptance, there is a tremendous and liberating freedom for both sides to confess, to be forgiven and then, with the matter resolved, to move on.

A happy home is one in which each spouse grants the possibility that the other may be right, though neither believes it.

Don Fraser

Because all Christians know (although they may need reminding!) that although they have done wrong things against God, they have been forgiven by him through Jesus, then this sort of free forgiveness should be something that is particularly characteristic of their marriages.

Now I will talk more about forgiveness in Chapter 4, but I want to say here that I acknowledge that forgiveness is not a soft option. It may be fairly easy to forgive when it's merely a case of 'sorry dear, I forgot to get the milk,' but it's much harder when it's something that has caused you emotional pain. And there are some cases (such as where unfaithfulness or abuse has occurred) where forgiveness is extremely hard indeed. And forgiveness (whether human or divine) should never be taken for granted. To say of some action 'oh that's all right, I'll be forgiven' is to abuse that relationship.

10. Beware of Complacency

Complacency is a deadly enemy of all marriages and is especially dangerous because it can creep into a relationship in a slow, subtle and undetected way. If you listen to those sad post-mortem statements people make about failed marriages you will often hear things like, 'I suppose we had come to take each other for granted.' 'I just assumed that . . .' or 'it just never occurred to me that . . .' It is a good principle in a marriage to be very wary of anything that can lead to complacency. Ironically, long-standing, successful marriages are more likely to be breeding grounds for complacency than troubled ones. In a marriage that has endured for years, it is easy to assume, because your relationship has survived so well and so long, that your future must be assured. That can be a dangerous mistake. Whatever the problems of being in a marriage that has gone through difficulties, there is much less danger of the couple concerned taking each other for granted.

How can you protect your marriage against such a subtle and invisible enemy as complacency? One way is to continue to watch your marriage and subject it to regular check-ups with your spouse to ensure that nothing has quietly crept in to alienate or annoy them. A more proactive

Some people pay a compliment as if they expect a receipt.

way is to work at appreciating your spouse. It is a sad fact that while familiarity may not breed contempt, it can certainly breed a carelessness that borders on contempt. It is all too easy to see or hear people being courteous to strangers while treating their spouse as if they were part of the furniture. It costs nothing to compliment your spouse or to thank them: whether it be for fixing the shower, taking the rubbish out or making dinner. And an unexpected gift at an unexpected time can make a spouse feel really special.

Beware complacency: look out for it and fight against it. Never take your spouse or your marriage for granted!

11. Stay Real

Many marriages get into trouble because an increasing but unseen gulf develops between what a marriage is believed to be and what the marriage really is. So, for example, he thinks that everything is fine while, in reality, his wife is going frantic trying to manage the new baby, or she imagines that there are no problems while her husband is increasingly losing his commitment to the relationship. This inability to see what is really going on, can be due either to a form of Rosy Romanticism[2] or to a wilful refusal to face up to the problems.

Without going around searching for problems in marriage – you may create them that way – it is important that you constantly check the health of your marriage, so that you see it as it really is, rather than how you think it is or would like it to be. That can be done by talking things through together, by going on marriage improvement seminars, or by reading good books on marriage. There are many parallels between marriage and flying a plane, not least, the fatal danger of losing the sense of where you are and where you are going. Many of the complex cockpit instruments of a modern aircraft are designed to relay the true state of the plane and to give warnings should it descend too low or drift into an unstable or dangerous mode of flying. Marriages need the psychological or spiritual equivalent of such sensors. It is all too easy for a marriage that seems to be on the right course to be, in reality, heading towards the ground.

Good friends can be a great help in enabling a married couple to stay real, and with other marriage issues as

[2] There are two main views that are commonly put forward about marriage – those of the Rosy Romantic (naive and optimistic) and the Cold Cynic (pessimistic, negative about the whole idea of whether traditional marriage can work).

well. There are two possibilities here. The first is where a married couple have an older married couple as friends, mentors and confidantes. The second is where each partner has a close friend of their own sex who they can fully trust and who can give them advice. Such friends, especially if they have been married for some time themselves, may (if they are close enough) be able to spot difficulties in a relationship before they emerge. It is sometimes easier to see other people's problems than your own.

12. Finally, Love in Every Way You Can

If you think of love only as romantic passion, then it is a relatively minor ingredient in the success of a marriage. If you think of love as the multifaceted thing that it really is, with

You can never be happily married to another until you get a divorce from yourself. A successful marriage demands a certain death to self.

Jerry McCant

all its aspects of craving, companionship, caring and commitment, then love is the great secret of a lasting and successful marriage. It summarises all those characteristics that keep a marriage going. While romantic passion cannot be controlled but only obeyed or resisted, the other aspects of love can be commanded. We can, and must, choose to love.

Let me here briefly touch on the four ingredients of love.

a) Craving Love

Of all the ingredients of love, craving love is the hardest to command. It is so linked to our hormones that some days we 'feel in love' with someone and some days we don't. Nevertheless, there is much that can be done to

keep craving love alive in a marriage. Let me suggest
three rules.

- Focus your love on your spouse. Quite simply, do all
  you can to try to think lovingly of your spouse.
  Dwell on their good points, try to overlook their bad
  ones, and remind yourself that they are your partner
  and you love them. Think of what is good about
  them and the good things that they have done. As
  the saying goes, accentuate the positive and
  eliminate the negative. And when romantic thoughts
  come to you about someone else, then resist and
  reject them.
- Work at being someone who can be loved by your
  spouse. If to focus your love onto your spouse is to
  work at desiring them, then you must also work at
  being desired by them. One of the many things in a
  marriage that should not be taken for granted is
  craving love. There are two opposing extreme views
  on how to retain your spouse's love. The first
  considers that looks and appearance are absolutely
  vital and the second, that looks and appearance
  don't matter. Subscribers to the first extreme view
  tend to spend heavily on smart clothes, make-up,
  hairdressing, the gym and, if they have the
  inclination and the money, cosmetic surgery.
  Subscribers to the second extreme view, instead,
  tend to slowly bulge or sag into a shambling and
  shabby old age. Both views are too extreme. Against
  the first view are the facts that pursuing the
  impossible goal of totally defeating the effects of
  time can be costly in more ways than one, and that it
  can distract from the relational side of a marriage.
  Against the second view is the fact that, while you
  can be loved because of your character, rather than

because of your looks, craving love does focus on appearance and can be dampened by carelessness towards appearance or hygiene. The middle route is wisest. Here, on the one hand, you care for how you look and you do your best to resist the ravages of time, kids and business lunches. But, to balance that, you also acknowledge that the heart of the relationship is not about the superficialities of looks and clothes. Work at desiring your spouse, but also work at being desirable.

- Keep the romance alive. There is a real danger in thinking that marriage marks an end to romance, and it is easy to become lax in this department. Business, chores and children can easily get in the way of a romantic life. Planning, creativity and commitment (and sometimes a lock to the bedroom door) may be needed to keep romance going. It may even take hard work to be romantic when you are tired or distracted. One of the myths of the age is that if you don't feel like something, then you don't have to do it. It is fatal advice in a marriage.

Craving love may be the hardest form of love to command and the most vulnerable to changes in mood, but to neglect it in a marriage is to cheat both yourself and your spouse: it is also (as we will see in Chapter 5) a way to prepare a fertile soil for an affair.

b) Companionship Love

Companionship can, and should, be developed in a marriage. Even if your spouse's interests are 'not your thing', do your best to develop a sympathy and understanding with them. So, if he is into rock climbing then, while you may decline to follow him up the cliff face, you might offer to carry some of the gear and sit nearby with a book (and try not to worry). And if she is interested in collecting old porcelain, he may choose to go round antique shops with her, put up some shelves for her collection and learn to distinguish Wedgwood from Delft.

It is, however, worth remembering that sharing activities is not always an automatic recipe for success. For instance, for a couple to play bridge together as a partnership may help bond a marriage, but if one partner bungles an important game then it can cause problems. Another example might be where one partner takes up the other's sport or pastime with enthusiasm and then excels at it to the extent that they become superior in it. It can require a great deal of grace to be beaten to second place in your sport by your own spouse! Another issue is that some people need their psychological space in a marriage and their Saturday morning's fishing or their piano playing may provide them with that.

One curious feature about companionship love is that it can actually be built up by negative events. So even if your holiday was a long tale of mishaps, the way that you handled it together may actually have strengthened the marriage. And disappointment and even tragedy can become something that unites rather than divides. Over the years, these bonds of shared trials and tribulations can build up to become part of the solid framework that holds a

My husband says he wants to spend his vacation someplace where he's never been before. I said, 'How about the kitchen?'

Nancy Tucket

marriage together. 'We've been through a lot together' is a phrase you often hear from those in long-standing marriages.

Finally, it is important to remember that companionship in a marriage can only occur where there is both communication and time allowed for it to develop.

c) Caring Love

When you think of caring or compassion love it is easy to concentrate on spectacular acts of caring, such as where a wife supports her husband psychologically during his quest for a new job, or he cares for her through a long and traumatic illness. Yet, to do this is to overlook the fact that most compassion love centres on day-to-day matters that are so small that we may consider them trivial. So, for instance, it is caring love that makes him clean the ice off the car in the winter mornings before she leaves for work and it is caring love that makes her mend his favourite sweater.

As with all the other elements of love, caring love involves both what is done and what is not done. So caring love may involve making an effort to encourage your spouse when they are going through a difficult time. But it is also caring love to refrain from criticising your spouse in public.

d) Commitment Love

Commitment love is the love that binds everything together. It is the sworn determination to seek the best for the other person, regardless of the cost. Sometimes commitment love is an act of the will against feelings. There may be days when you will not like what your spouse said or did, when your feelings are of anger, hurt, disgust or disappointment, but it is then that commitment love comes into its own, as your determination to keep your promises overrules those feelings.

With enough commitment love on both sides, almost any marriage will endure. It might not be exciting, and almost certainly it wouldn't be the stuff of dreams or

sizzling novels, but it would survive. But the other side of
the coin is that once commitment love falters, even in a
marriage with a lot of other things going for it, then the storm clouds are gathering.

*While the marriage vow
cannot guarantee that we
will always handle
everything that comes up, it
does signal our intention to
make the attempt.*

John Welwood

The key to remaining committed is to regularly remind yourself that you have made promises of commitment. The real significance of a wedding ring is not that it is a signal to other people that you are 'already taken', it is a visible and permanent reminder of the vows of commitment that you have made.

Wedding anniversaries are a good excuse for a celebration, but they are also a good opportunity for a couple to remind themselves of their wedding vows. For a Christian, vows are important: after all, our whole faith is founded on God making and keeping his sworn promises to us. Those of us who have trusted in God's faithfulness to his promises should be people whose priority is to keep the promises we have ourselves made.

These then are the 12 great principles of marriage. In the next two chapters we will see how they are employed in the practice of marriage so that the two do indeed become one.

Chapter 2

The Practice of Marriage (2)
The Sexual Dimension

Steve looked out of the window and decided that it was warm enough to risk eating his lunch outside. He put aside the barrister's notes for the forthcoming Macpherson trial, then walked down through the cramped labyrinth of passageways that ran through the solicitors' offices, out to the small patch of grass at the back. Elsie Taylor, who had been secretary of Wills and Probate for as long as anyone could remember, was sitting on one of the two benches, carefully finishing an apple and reading a newspaper.

They exchanged greetings.

'So what's in your paper?' Steve asked.

She flicked a finger at the cover of the tabloid, 'Sex.'

'I thought that was yesterday?'

'And tomorrow and the day after. It's overrated isn't it?'

Steve paused. 'Compared to what?'

Elsie looked at him over her glasses with mock severity, 'When you and your Melanie have been married the 30 years Ted and I have, you'll learn. Overrated.' She gave him a wink.

'I'll let you know,' Steve said, deciding that with 28 years left to run, it was a safe promise to make.

When, a few minutes later, Elsie left, leaving Steve alone in the late April sun, her verdict on sex came back to his mind. 'After two years of marriage, what is my evaluation?' he wondered. 'My client, Sex,' he thought, 'stands accused of being overrated. How would I make a defence?'

As he chewed slowly through his sandwiches, he tried to summarise his feelings. The whole sex thing seemed such a mass of contradictions that a conclusion was surprisingly hard. For every statement he could make, there also seemed to be an opposite one. Certainly, sex was powerful. At times, his desire for Melanie had such strength that he felt an uneasy empathy with those pathetic clients who muttered, 'I couldn't help myself.' And yet, at other times, it bordered on a duty, and at still others any desire was absent altogether. There seemed to be no rhyme or reason. And sex was romantic, of course ... or was it? Sometimes it was down-to-earth, matter of fact and devoid of any real romantic edge. In fact, Steve realised that he wasn't even sure whether it was comforting or unsettling. He felt himself frown as he decided that it could be both. On balance, whatever sex was, it was not overrated.

'Deep in thought Steve?'

Steve was suddenly aware that the elegant, dark-suited Stuart Barker was standing next to him.

'Sorry Stu, didn't see you. I was ...' Steve paused, 'pondering a case.'

'And is the client guilty or innocent?'

'Oh, guilty. But probably not of this particular charge.'

Introduction

This chapter and the next are closely linked to Chapter 1. Whereas that chapter suggested some principles by which a marriage can be built up and maintained, these two chapters look in more depth at how a marriage works in practice. The basis of marriage is bonding, so that a good marriage is an arrangement where, without losing their own individuality, two people become one.

But what actually is it that bonds a marriage? Is it a similar temperament? Shared interests? Good sex? I think that, in reality, the best marriages are not held together by any one single thing, but instead, by countless little bonds generated over the years. In such a marriage, it is as though a vast web of tiny threads ties the husband and wife together. Every time the couple successfully engage in conversation, do something together, hold hands, kiss, or express appreciation, then another new bonding thread is spun between them. And every row and disagreement breaks or weakens these bonds.

In the following pages, I want to talk about this bonding and to make some suggestions on how this can best be achieved and sustained. The framework I want to use to look at it is the four dimensions or bonds of marriage: the social, psychological, sexual and the spiritual. In this chapter, I want to deal exclusively with the sexual side of marriage. The three other dimensions will be covered in the next chapter. Here, I want to make amends by putting it first and devoting a whole chapter to it.

The sexual aspect of marriage is not only one that is very important, it is also one where there is an enormous amount of mythology. In this chapter, I want to try to dispel some of these myths and then to suggest a number of guidelines that will help create and enhance the sexual side of a marriage.

At the start, I need to explain that what I cover here are general aspects of sexual relations rather than the technical, biological or even medical specifics. There are two reasons for this emphasis. One, I do not have the training to be able to cover the physical side of sex in detail. In fact, this area of marriage has suffered badly from the ill-informed advice of enthusiastic, self-appointed experts and it is worth emphasising that, in the case of a genuine problem, it is important to get advice from someone who has proper medical qualifications. Two, as I will explain below, while I have no doubt that there is ignorance on sexual matters in our society, I think the real area of ignorance is not that of the mechanics of sexual intercourse, but of

> *Literature is mostly about having sex and not much about having children; life is the other way round.*
>
> **David Lodge**

how sexual relationships work. Our society is reminiscent of someone who knows absolutely everything about the internal combustion engine, but has not learned how to drive a car. In a similar way, people today know everything about sex except those things that are truly important: we have produced a generation that knows all about the clitoris and almost nothing about commitment.

Before outlining some specific guidelines on sex, I want to look at the long-standing and persistent allegation that Christianity is anti-sex. The philosopher Bertrand Russell (1872–1970) may be taken as typical in this respect. One of his many comments on the subject was this, 'The worst feature of the Christian religion . . . is its attitude towards sex – an attitude so morbid and so unnatural . . .'[1] Let me make four responses.

1. The Christian view of sex is, in fact, highly positive. Christians believe that sex is a gift from God and, within the social and psychological framework of marriage, a rich blessing. The Bible constantly celebrates sex within marriage and a whole book of the Bible, the Song of Songs (also called the Song of Solomon) is devoted to praising sexual love. Of

[1] 'Has Religion Made Useful Contributions to Civilization?' *Philosophical Entrées: Classic and Contemporary Readings in Philosophy* Part 4, Ed. Jacquette.

course, Christians have protested against sex outside marriage, but those objections are similar to those of someone who protests about a great work of art being trivialised: it is a protest precisely because we value the thing which is being abused. Sadly, there have been Christian thinkers (some of them influential) who have been unenthusiastic about sex, even in marriage, but in taking such a view they have gone against the Bible's teaching. In fact, if you want a truly anti-sex religion, try Buddhism: there, the goal of existence is the extinction of all passions and cravings.

2. In reality, many of the attacks on the Christian attitude to sex seem to have had ulterior motives. In particular, there have been a large number of people whose battles against Christian sexual ethics have been driven either by a need to justify their own sexual appetites or a desire to 'liberate' particular individuals from chastity or marital faithfulness. For example, Bertrand Russell, who I quoted earlier, had an almost insatiable sexual appetite that led to four unhappy marriages, many mistresses and a vast number of affairs. His attacks on Christian sexual ethics hardly come from a neutral standpoint.

3. With the increasing awareness of the problems of paedophilia, sexual abuse, harassment and sexual addiction, there is a growing awareness of the 'dark side' of sexuality. Even the most liberated of people now accept that there have to be some rules.

4. Finally, not only are Christians pro-sex in theory, all the evidence suggests that they are also pro-sex in practice. Studies suggest that Christian marriages remain sexually active longer and maintain a higher level of satisfaction than non-Christian ones. When, in 1994, University of Chicago researchers released the survey results on personal beliefs and quality of

sex, it showed that women with theologically conservative Protestant beliefs reported the most orgasms by far: 32 per cent said that they achieve orgasm every time they make love. 'Mainline Protestants' and Catholics lagged five points behind, and those people with 'no religious affilia-tion' were at 22 per cent. It could perhaps be said that, if it wasn't for the noise of creaking bedsprings, you could probably hear the sound of Christians having the last laugh!

Eight Guidelines

Let me suggest eight guidelines to do with sex in marriage. Some of them are closely linked to the general principles for marriage that I outlined in the previous chapter. This should hardly be surprising; after all, the sexual dimension of marriage obeys the same rules as the rest of marriage.

1. Set your own standards

Our society has very firm values about sex and seems to use every opportunity to impose them on others. When combined, these values actually amount to a great myth that seems to be created as follows.

a) Everybody has sex.
b) Everybody enjoys great sex.
c) Everybody enjoys great sex all of the time.
d) Everybody enjoys great sex all of the time in a succession of incredibly varied and athletic ways.
e) Everybody enjoys great sex all of the time in a succession of incredibly varied and athletic ways from the first time they make love.

The principle that I want to put forward here is this: when faced with all or part of this myth (*lie* might be a more honest word) I suggest that you just ignore it. Set your own standard. The best rule for married sex is this: find out what works for you both and do it, whenever and however you please. Don't worry about what everyone else is claiming that they do, or how frequently they claim that they are doing it.[2] If you have discovered something that brings both of you intimacy, satisfaction

Women complain about sex more often than men. Their gripes fall into two major categories: (1) Not enough; (2) Too much.

Ann Landers

and pleasure then well done, rejoice and keep going. This is not to suggest that you ignore real and genuine problems – I will look at those later – but I do advise that you shouldn't take all you hear as a standard.

There is another implication of setting your own standard: if things aren't that wonderful in the sexual area of your marriage, don't make things worse by imagining that only you have such problems. In particular, don't expect wonders from the first night of a honeymoon.

2. Take your time

Linked to setting your own standard is the need to set your own pace. In particular, aim for the long term, not the short. We live in an age where everything must be done by today and every conceivable way is found to speed things up. But achieving good sex is something that, like the making of a good wine or growing a tree, cannot be rushed – it cannot be 'microwaved'. Quite

---

[2] It may not be true anyway. No human activity is more associated with lies than sex.

simply, it may take time to find out your spouse's likes
and dislikes. In fact, attempts to speed things up can
make things worse.

Actually, taking time is not the problem that people
portray it as. One of the best kept secrets of life is that
good sex can continue well into old age. Yes, it may
change, but such changes may not necessarily be for the
worse. For example, any reduction in the frequency of sex
with age may be more than compensated for by increased
skill and knowledge. So taking time to adjust to your
spouse's wants and needs should not be an issue. With
the possibility of 40 years of great sex ahead, why hurry?

This pacing of the sexual relationship may not only be
needed during the early days of marriage, it may also be
appropriate later. For instance, during pregnancy, and
possibly for some time afterwards, a woman may neither
be able to have full intercourse nor desire it. The sensitive
husband will adjust his demands accordingly.

3. Avoid the pressure for performance

While our culture pretends that sex is merely a bit of fun,
there is, at depth, a worried seriousness about it. Endless
books and magazine articles suggest that 'sexual fulfilment' is the ultimate meaning of existence and therefore
needs to be zealously worked
at. The result is an extraordinary emphasis on per-
formance and technique. This
stress on performance casts a
shadow over the marriage bed. The pressure is on and you
have to deliver – nothing less than a 100 per cent orgasm
rate is good enough. Mind you, if you do not subscribe to a
philosophy of lifelong permanent marriage, a poor sexual
performance may well be a matter for concern: failure

> *Sex is hereditary. If your
> parents never had it,
> chances are you won't
> either.*

could result in you being dropped for a better-performing model.

Yet there is a curious (and, to my mind, amusing) irony here. To treat sex as an Olympic sport can actually be self-defeating. It is generally agreed that sexual performance is not improved by pressure and to frantically seek more can often result in achieving much less. Now I am not defending poor or clumsy sexual technique. But I do think that there is a lot to be said for treating the textbooks on technique with much caution (and a degree of humour). My own advice to newly-weds would be to start by taking your time and having fun together without consulting the books. The old rule of 'if it ain't bust don't fix it' applies to sex as well as a lot of other things. Actually, as a Christian, I vaguely resent the suggestion in many articles that to have good sex requires, if not a doctorate in sexual physiology, at least a 200-page book. It implies that God blundered by making the parts without supplying the instruction manual to go with them.

One of the great things about the sort of lifelong, permanent marriage that I am defending throughout this book, is that the pressure for sexual performance is lifted. There is space for fun, relaxation, laughter and even failure. There is certainly no place for a critical preoccupation with how well you are doing. In fact, the freedom to fail that there is within marriage is both enormously liberating and ultimately contributes to a higher quality of sex. Your times of sex will be most satisfying (and most fun) if they are free from anxiety and demand.

4. Get the right attitude to sex

As I have indicated, it is easy to have wrong attitudes towards sex. In fact, our culture is in a total mess about the whole subject. For example, on the one hand, it says that sex is simply another bodily function and there should be 'no taboos' about it. Yet, on the other, it acknowledges that sex is special because of the way it uses it to sell magazines, cars and almost everything else.

In this sea of conflicting and contradictory attitudes to sex, what are we to think? Let me suggest that there are some attitudes that any married couple should take on board.

a) Honour sex in your marriage

Some people have negative views on sex, even in marriage. It is not just people who come from confining and repressive backgrounds who can assume this attitude. There are also those who, because they have been so overexposed to sex, have become jaded and bored with the whole thing.

It is important to remember that, in marriage, sex is good. The Christian's view of sex is that it is as much a gift from God as food or drink is – it is something to be thankful for.

The idea that sex is a gift from God also counters the danger of considering sex, even in marriage, as somehow shameful. Many people assume that only those with traditional attitudes can consider sex as shocking or shameful: yet things are not so simple. Despite the fact that our modern, secular society claims to have a free and open mind on the matter of sex, negative attitudes to it are still present. For instance, note the adjective used in such phrases as 'talking dirty' and 'dirty jokes'. In fact, most 'adult humour' is based on the assumption that there is something about sex that we should snigger over. The fact is that in marriage, sex is not shameful – it is positively honourable. It is also something that a husband and wife should be able to talk freely to each other about.

Ironically, if one result of honouring or valuing sex is to

allow it to be freely talked about within a marriage, another result is to keep it private. The sexual relationship between a man and a wife is something that is so intimate that it lies at the very heart of what a marriage is. Because of that, it needs to be protected, and one means of protecting it is to surround it with privacy. This needs emphasising because it is often assumed that some people (and Christians in particular) do not talk about sex because they are ashamed of it. In fact, the real motive for silence is respect, not shame. Because the sexual relationship between a couple is so intimate, their sexual achievements or failures are not a public matter.

> *Traditionally, sex has been a very private, secretive activity. Herein perhaps lies its powerful force for uniting people in a strong bond. As we make sex less secretive, we may rob it of its power to hold men and women together.*
>
> **Thomas Szasz**

b) Integrate sex into your marriage

There is a real danger in a marriage that sex is somehow isolated from all other aspects of being married. This is easy to do: after all, your sex life is something private, in a way that the other aspects of a marriage are not. But to treat it as some sort of separate, add-on phenomenon, rather than an integral part of a marriage is dangerous. You need to remember that you are not just a married couple who, every so often, have a specific activity called 'sex', you are a married couple whose marriage has a sexual aspect that affects everything that you are.

I will talk more about gender attitudes to sex but, in different ways, both sexes need to know that sex is a central aspect of a marriage and not some 'optional extra' that can be isolated. A man may need to realise that he cannot have a blazing row with his wife and then expect sex with her, as if their argument was irrelevant. And a woman cannot expect to have the companionship and affection she wants from her husband, while denying him sex. Furthermore, to treat sex as something separate or peripheral to the heart of a marriage is to provide a favourable setting for an affair. After all, a man might say, as he visits a prostitute, that his sexual life and his marriage are two separate things.

Some Christians face a particular problem of seeming to separate the sexual side of their marriage from their spiritual life. Behind this may lie a lingering belief that, even in marriage, sex is somehow wrong or sinful. If this applies to you, then you may need to do some hard thinking. God gave sex for marriage: rejoice, enjoy and be grateful.

There is more that could be written about how to value sex and integrate it into a marriage. But these right attitudes are worth working to achieve. After all, our attitudes control our actions. To know that sex is an honoured, valuable and integral part of marriage is to set the stage for a passionate, erotic and lasting relationship.

5. Cultivate good sex

> *You mustn't force sex to do the work of love or love to do the work of sex.*
>
> **Mary McCarthy**

I would call this guideline 'work at sex' but that conjures up those grim (and very unerotic) articles that are entitled 'Twenty Exercises to Improve Your Sexual Performance' or 'Workout Techniques to Spice Up Your Love Life'. The fact is, though, that a great and fulfilling sex life in a marriage doesn't just happen: it is something that needs to be cultivated and nurtured. And, as in other areas of marriage, it is something that may require sustained effort.

There are a number of issues here, but let me highlight some of the most major.

a) Be prepared to learn

As the vast numbers of teenage pregnancies suggest, you don't need training to have sex. But to make the most out of the lifelong sexual relationship that lies at the heart of marriage does require an ability to learn. That learning may come from two sources.

The main source of learning should come from your own spouse. Learn what they enjoy and listen to what they say. Here, as elsewhere, good communication is vital. A second source of learning can be books and articles on sex. These fall into two basic groups. One group, potentially helpful, includes many good semi-technical books on sex, written by people who know what they are talking about. If you are really short of knowledge in this area then they may be very useful.[3] But the other group of books and articles are very different and are capable of doing far more harm than good. Some of them are little more than pornography disguised as education or advice. Others are deeply misleading in their suggestions that great sex can only be achieved by mastering exotic techniques or by finding the 'right person'. Again, don't believe everything you read, and be discerning. Any advice that does not make psychological intimacy, communication and love in all its forms central is unlikely to be helpful, whatever short-term benefits it yields.

b) Make sex a priority

To most newly-weds, the idea of making sex a priority must seem a strange concept: after all, their problem is making a priority of anything else. Here, however, lies

---

[3] For example, *The Magic of Sex* by Dr Miriam Stoppard. From a specifically Christian viewpoint see *The Act of Marriage: The Beauty of Sexual Love* by Tim and Beverley Lahaye, and *Intended for Pleasure*, Ed and Gaye Wheat.

the problem. It is easy for newly married people to assume that sex is something that, by its nature, will always force itself onto the agenda of any marriage: you don't need to make time for sex, it can do that by itself. Yet even natural things need a helping hand occasionally and the fact is that as time goes by, the sexual side of a marriage can be put under pressure. Children, work, tiredness, a lack of time: all these things may combine to squeeze out sexual encounters.

The answer is to take action to ensure that the sexual relationship with your spouse continues. It is another myth that good sex is always spontaneous and 'just happens'. It may do (and if it does, great), but in practice, it frequently requires some effort to make it happen. So make dates with each other, go to bed early, postpone or reject commitments that will eat into time together. Try not to get too tired for lovemaking. There are other suggestions that can be made to improve a sex life. Keeping physically fit is an excellent recommendation, so skip watching TV, and go for a long walk together instead. Maintaining proper care of your body and practising good hygiene are also important ways in which you can make sex a priority and show that you care for and respect your spouse.

Do remember though that, while sex must be one of the basics of marriage, you must be careful lest it become the basis of marriage. Sexual desire is too changeable and capricious a substance to be the only foundation of your marriage.

c) Understand gender differences

In the previous chapter I talked about how men and women differ in terms of how they think and how they behave. These differences are particularly prominent in the area of sex, and understanding them helps in establishing a great sexual relationship in a marriage. Let me list some of the differences that have been identified.

> *For a woman there is nothing more erotic than being understood.*
> **Molly Haskell**

- Women view sex as the physical expression of an intimate, tender, stable and committed relationship. In contrast, while men can see things this way, they are able to separate sex from the rest of the relationship and to treat it as primarily, or even solely, a physical event.
- The pattern of sexual arousal differs markedly between the sexes. Arousal happens quickly with men, but fades rapidly after orgasm. In contrast, while arousal in women happens far more slowly, it is maintained for longer.
- In general, men can be aroused by visual stimuli, while women are aroused more by words, touch and atmosphere.
- Men desire more frequent and more varied sex than women do. Woman value consistency more than they do variety.

Of course, there are exceptions to these rules, but the principles are generally valid. Both sexes (but men in particular) overlook these differences and assume that their spouse functions and responds sexually in the same way that they do. These differences can be a stumbling block to the best possible sexual relationship, yet they can also be an enormous opportunity for a couple to show each other respect and love as they identify with, and respond to, their spouse's needs. The rule is this: don't just be content with what works for you, put your spouse first.

d) Beware of complacency

In many marriages, a good sex life begins during the honeymoon and, without effort or intervention, stays

> *Each coming together of man and wife, even if they have been mated for many years, should be a fresh adventure; each winning should necessitate a fresh wooing.*
>
> **Marie Stopes**

good and gets even better as time passes. But marriages like these, although very fortunate, can be particularly susceptible to complacency. Because the couple concerned have always taken sex for granted, they fail to take action when things start to slowly deteriorate. In fact, they may be so confident and unworried that they totally fail to notice that things in bed are no longer what they were.

Without encouraging the neurotic attitude that I condemned earlier, of worriedly logging the frequency and quality of your every sexual encounter together, it is worth making sure that you are neither taking sex nor each other for granted. There may be room for improvement. Try some changes in your routine; vary position, pace, timing or location. Don't let boredom get a look in.

6. Keep love in lovemaking

'Making love' is a modern euphemism for sex, but the sad reality is that love (except in the form of a very limited type of craving love) can, when it comes to sex, often be conspicuous by its absence. One of the many unfortunate aspects of our culture's attitude to sex has been to focus attention on the purely physical issues of technique and performance at the expense of relationship issues. The result is shallow, short-term and frequently unsatisfactory relationships outside marriage that can barely even merit the term 'romances'. Such attitudes can also spill over into marriage, and to counter them it is important to remember that sexual desire should not be separated from those other ingredients of love: caring, companionship and commitment love. Linked with them, sexual desire can flourish and grow for years, but detached from them, it soon degenerates to lust.

How do you keep love in your lovemaking? Practically, sex can be kept physically linked to love by continued contact such as kissing, hugging and embracing. Whilst men may see such things as affection rather than sex, for women affection is part of sex. Sex can be kept psychologically linked to love through conversation, sharing, and by giving each other the attention each needs.

One very practical way to keep love in married lovemaking is to keep dating. Your dates don't need to be exactly what they were before you were married. In fact, you may be able to meet each other's needs without actually 'going out'. But if you stay in, your time together can all too easily become eroded by personal projects, phone calls, visitors or email. Go out if you can, and if you do go out, switch your mobile off.

The mind can also be an erogenous zone.

Raquel Welch

Let me make a final comment here. Keeping love and lovemaking linked is beneficial to both the relationship and the sex in that relationship. After all, at the heart of love lies a desire to put the other person first. And I don't think it takes much imagination to see that a sexual relationship where two people are intent on giving is going to be better than one where both are intent on taking.

7. Have freedom and set limits

A curious aspect of the human race is its desire to have precisely defined limits. At least part of this desire seems to be a perverse wish to have these boundaries defined just so that we can rebelliously put a toe over them. Significantly, the issue of boundary drawing within marriage is not just one for the Christian: for all their talk of freedom, even the most liberal minds can come up with lists of such sexually unacceptable behaviour as rape, paedophilia, incest and bestiality. The fact is that all but the most naive admit that there are aspects to human sexual desire that need to be kept at bay.

But are there boundaries, and where do we put them? Before suggesting some guidelines here I want to be positive. Within marriage there is a vast area of mutual behaviour that can be considered 'legitimate sexual expression' and which is free for exploration. Even with vast amounts of time, energy, ingenuity and athleticism, a couple aren't likely to exhaust the possibilities that are there for the taking. If you put loving your spouse first and see sex as a way of expressing that love and the oneness of your marriage, the idea of finding limits or boundaries will be largely irrelevant.

Nevertheless, some comment on where the boundaries lie must be made. I think the limits around sexual freedom in marriage are defined by two criteria: what is not loving and what is harmful. The first criterion of love comes out of the biblical command to love your spouse. In sex, as elsewhere, you are to desire the best for them. It means that whatever is practised in a marriage has to be mutually agreed upon and that no party in a marriage should insist on anything that the other is not happy with. To do that is coercion, intimidation or worse. It is not love. By the way, although

Erotic practices have been diversified. Sex used to be a single-crop farming, like cotton or wheat, now people raise all sorts of things.

Saul Bellow

its proponents might not realise it, the modern secular concept of 'consensual sex' derives from this Christian principle – that sex should be consensual is not a principle built into human beings: after all, in some cultures and ethical systems a husband has an absolute right over his wife.

To apply the limit of 'what is not loving' to sexual behaviour is, I think, fairly straightforward. The second criterion of 'what is harmful' is more complex because there are different sorts of harm. Thus, some practices can be ruled out in a marriage because of the health hazards involved. But harm can be inflicted in other ways. The use of pornography or sexual fantasies can be harmful, because both of these activities can be enslaving. They are also potentially harmful because fantasising about someone other than your spouse can be the first step to betraying your marriage vows. The distance between mental and physical adultery is a shorter one than many people think. If there must be fantasies, keep them spouse-centred. The idea of spicing up your sex life is fine, but sometimes the choice of spice can be dangerous.

Another temptation can be to use sex in a marriage as a reward, a weapon or an instrument of manipulation. He may say he's 'not feeling like it' because he's annoyed with her because she won't let him go to the football. And she may use sex to sweeten him up to agree to some ambitious holiday plans. This sort of misuse of sex is not only wrong, it sets a dangerous precedent; what was meant to unite is used to divide.[4]

---

[4] In fact, although there is very little New Testament advice specifically on marital sex (as opposed to a lot of general principles), the withholding of sex is condemned by the Apostle Paul in 1 Corinthians 7:5 'So do not deprive each other of sexual relations.'

8. Handle problems properly

The last guideline that I want to suggest involves the handling of sexual problems. Because sex is so powerful a force and so integral to the heart of any relationship, when sexual problems occur they can be very destructive. I want to briefly discuss here two sorts of problems: those of the past and those of the present.

a) Past problems

In the area of sex, many people have a past that is either painful, shameful or both. One person may have suffered sexual abuse, another may have a history of promiscuity and still another may feel guilt over the sexual hurts they have inflicted on others. For something that so many people consider merely harmless fun, sex has an extraordinary ability to inflict appalling wounds.

Now giving general advice in this area of sexual pain or guilt is hard because of the complexities of the issues involved. After all, someone might have been victim, perpetrator or both. The issues may be relatively minor, such as guilty feelings about having been involved in some now regretted adolescent relationship, or they may be serious enough to have legal implications. Three general points can, however, be made:

- First, these issues must be faced. It is a widely believed fallacy that time alone will bring healing. The sad fact is that, generally speaking, time will not heal something as fundamental as sexual hurt. It may simply bury the matter, only for it to surface and cause problems years later. An experience of sexual abuse, promiscuity, rape, or some sexual addiction in the past, can make it hard, sometimes even impossible, to enjoy sexual intimacy subsequently. The wisest thing to do is to find someone who is a trained counsellor and talk things through honestly with them.

- Second, (and here I unrepentantly adopt a Christian standpoint) I am convinced that, despite the fact that sexual ordeals or problems are far from trivial, a very large measure of healing, forgiveness and restoration is possible. You may feel that what was done to you in the past is something that is fixed, permanent and binding, but the great news of Christianity is that through Jesus Christ there is healing, cleansing and freedom.

- Third, if it emerges that it is your spouse who has problems in this area, then be sympathetic, unshockable and encourage them to seek assistance, however painful it might be.[5]

b) Present problems

I have already suggested that the sexual relationship in a marriage may not be an instant, explosive success. My advice, which I repeat here, is not to worry and to take your time. If, after a few weeks or months there are still problems, then do some reading around. And if that doesn't work, then some counselling may be a good way forward.

Equally, after years of having a good sexual relationship, a couple may suddenly hit a spot where he or she is unable to deliver what is required. Here, not only is counselling a good idea, but also a talk with a sympathetic doctor would help. The human sexual drive

---

[5] If the issues that emerge involve potentially criminal offences then, however tempting it may be, do not try to cover the matter up. To be involved in concealing a crime is to assist it. Find a trustworthy and sensitive counsellor and explain the situation; they will give advice on how the matter may best be taken forward.

is very susceptible to changes in the body's overall wellbeing, and a decline in sexual interest or ability may reflect some hormonal or other metabolic problem. And if your sexual problems are due to something like high blood pressure or diabetes, then no amount of counselling is going to cure the problem. If the problem is purely one of a sexual malfunction, be encouraged, there is now a great deal of medical success in the treatment of such problems.

When the sexual side of a marriage is not working well, it is tempting to dodge the real issue. People in general, and men in particular, often prefer not to admit that there is a problem. The result, however, may be that fear, anger, shame or guilt build up. And, in that sort of environment, things can get worse.

It is always worth remembering that although everything may be fine now, things may change. Avoid complacency and be careful about letting sex become the central focus of your marriage. Above all, work at sex: emphasise it as the giving of pleasure and talk to each other about it. Remember, when you get it right, sex can be a tremendous and God-given asset to a marriage and a wonderful expression of love.

Chapter 3

The Practice of Marriage (3)
The Social, Psychological and Spiritual Dimensions

It was mid-morning before Cathy finally got Patrick to go to sleep. Exhausted, but determined not to sleep herself, Cathy closed the door on the baby's bedroom and tiptoed downstairs, shivering as she glimpsed the rain lashing against the glass of the front door.

As ever, there was housework to be done, and postponing the vacuuming for fear of waking Patrick, Cathy turned to dusting. As she wiped the photograph of her wedding that hung on the living room wall she stopped and stared at it. Three years ago and a world away, she thought – how promising it had all seemed then. Gary had been a wonderful catch and his job had seemed so promising. Her career looked secure and there had been those hints from her Uncle Ryan about help towards a mortgage. God had been in his heaven, all had been right with the world and the sun had shone above them. She shook her head and sighed quietly. Like Uncle Ryan's imagined wealth, it all seemed to have faded away. Their lives had gone from that sun-drenched June day to this storm-blown November.

Struck by the way her dreams had been drained of fulfilment, she looked around her. The room, like the rest of the house, was small and, for all her efforts, still looked shabby. She tried not to notice how the damp patch below the window seemed to have spread further.

She stared at the photo again. How young Gary looked then! Commuting had taken its toll. He was tired and grumpy for most of the week and really only recovered by Saturday night. They barely had time to talk these days and both of them were so tired that when they did have time, either they didn't talk, or when they did they disagreed. He was perhaps, she felt, not the man she had married; he was colder and more distant. And their social life was a joke. The housing estate was unfriendly and, although the church was helpful, no one seemed to live near them. Of course Gary had the car during the day and in the evenings he was generally too exhausted, or simply back too late for them to get out. And babysitters were hard to get. It was easy to blame Patrick's unexpected arrival on the scene for some of the issues, but he was only part of the problem.

For a moment, Cathy felt a spasm of sadness for herself. Then she shook her head in determination. Nevertheless, she said to herself, I chose Gary and he chose me. I have a home, a husband and a child, and I will count my blessings. God is still in his heaven, even if all is not right with the world.

And she realised that she was smiling.

Introduction

In the last chapter, I considered the sexual dimension of marriage. In this chapter, I want to look at the three remaining dimensions: the social, the psychological and the spiritual. I do, however, need to say that although boundaries between these dimensions do exist, they are not rigidly defined and there is overlap. For instance, being shy in the psychological dimension will almost certainly have consequences in the social dimension. And Christians will say that the spiritual dimension cannot be isolated as it affects every aspect of life and marriage.

The Social Dimension of Marriage

A newly-married couple are a totally new social unit and they need to learn to operate as a new family.

Creating a new family

It is vital to understand that a married couple are not simply two people living together in a long-term sexual union recognised by society – they are something much more. They are part of an entirely new family unit. In this respect (as in others), living together is mis-leading and short-changes its practitioners. Marriage involves a very much deeper level of sharing and commitment and, not only is living together not the real thing; it is not even a good preparation for the real thing.

> *Families ain't just born, you got to work at 'em, even when there ain't much to work with.*
>
> **Marsha Hunt**

Being a new social unit is not something that happens automatically when people get married. Like all other areas of a marriage, it is something that needs to be worked at, talked through, planned and implemented. In addition, there are pressures, often from well-intentioned friends and family, which need to be resisted.

Breaking free of the past

Part of becoming a new and autonomous family is making a break with the past. With a marriage everything becomes new. Past links with family and friends, and social habits must all be re-examined in the light of the new family unit that has been created.

One notorious problem area involves dealing with parents. Problems can be inflicted upon a marriage when, for instance, one parent feels that a son or daughter's marriage needs their help and the benefit of their wise counsel and experience. The consequence is, the intrusion of one generation into the lives of the next generation, and the long-term consequences are rarely happy. Somehow, tactfully and delicately, boundaries have to be drawn. The old saying to parents, which is often trotted out at weddings, is that it is 'not so much losing a son as gaining a daughter' (or vice versa). Well that may be true, but it should not obscure the reality that parents must agree to a real letting go in terms of authority and influence. Wise parents will leave a clear and well-defined space between themselves and their children's marriage.

Yet it is not always the parents who are to blame. Sometimes they can be dragged in, often against their better judgement, when someone in a marriage fails to separate themselves from their biological family. So, for example, it is a dangerous habit for a husband to talk to his mother about his marital problems rather than resolving them with his wife. And if, every time there is a row, a wife goes back to her parents, then that can make matters much worse. It is a good general guideline that if one partner is alone with their parents they should not say anything that could not be said with their spouse present. It can cause problems when someone has previously had their father or mother as their confidante: if they continue this into the marriage their spouse is likely to feel threatened, and if they stop it the parent may feel aggrieved. This is a conflict of loyalties that needs handling sensitively, but the general principle still holds: when you are married, your spouse comes before your parents.

There can also be issues to do with criticism of parents or families. A husband may find that, although his wife says rude things about her own mother, if he agrees with them this may be coolly received and be seen as an attack on her family. If both generations handle it properly, the relationship between a married couple and their parents can be a great blessing all round. Mishandled, it can do a lot of damage. And, of course, as has often been noted that while you can get new friends, you can't change your family.

Old friends and social activities can also pose problems, though to a lesser extent. So whether, once married, he continues to go out with his mates every Friday and she persists in having her friends round every Tuesday evening, are matters that ought to be looked at carefully. Such social events may provide a welcome breathing space for both partners or they may impose stresses on the marriage. Examine, communicate, discuss and resolve together.

Creating new patterns

But there is more to creating a new family than just separating from the past. A marriage is also an opportunity to make a fresh start. New patterns should be established, and these may range from the routine and trivial (such as who puts out the rubbish and who does the washing-up), to much bigger issues such as who takes on the responsibility for finances and budgeting. These are all matters that must be talked through and agreed together. There is no reason to assume that what worked well for your parents will also work well for you.

Incidentally, although I support what I call 'traditional marriages' do not assume that I (or Christians generally) also support tradition when it comes to such things as household roles. My support for traditional marriage is because it is, very largely, based on God's definitive pattern for human life as revealed in the Bible. There is no similar teaching on such things like household roles, and I see nothing wrong in 'house-husbands' and wives earning most of the income in a household. There may be issues to do with how the psychological, social and spiritual dynamics of a family works in specific cases, but in principle at least I see no problem.

In many marriages, there is a division of authority and responsibility between the couple depending on gifts and interests. So, because she has a talent for figures, she balances the books and because he is skilled with his hands, he does all the fixing of things around the house. At its best, this works well, avoiding duplication of effort and helping to integrate the husband and wife into the new unity of the marriage. In some marriages, such an interlocking of the husband and wife is so major that the idea of them splitting up becomes almost impossible to visualise because they have become totally dependent on each other.

Although this division of responsibilities is generally a good thing, there are some dangers. When it works well, it works very well; when it works badly, it can be catastrophic. Things can slip through the gap ('I thought you were managing this') or people can feel edged out ('I'm never consulted'). Furthermore, this division of labour can be an excuse to revert to traditional roles that may be neither wise nor appropriate today. And when illness or death affects the marriage, such a policy can cause problems as it may then be hard for one person to run the whole household on their own. Also, there are some big issues, such as how much money is spent against how much is saved, how children are disciplined and so on, that must be shared decisions. And even when you have allocated spheres of responsibility, it is still a good idea to ask each other's opinion. It is a good way of showing mutual respect.

One positive aspect of being married and starting a new family is that you can start new traditions. So a couple may sit down and discuss together the traditions and rituals that they used to celebrate birthdays, Christmas, New Year and so on in their families. They then decide together which to adopt or whether to start their own traditions.

Part of this social dimension is the need to create a home. For a married couple, a home is more than just a place where they live. It is, or ought to be, a place that is, in some way, an extension of who they are as a couple. Just as an artist's painting is an expression of who he or she is, so a couple's house expresses who they are and what they stand for. Whether it is a tiny flat that you rent or a sprawling, well-furnished house that you own, where you live needs to be more than four walls and furniture. It needs to be a home.

Financial issues

One area of marriage is so important that it needs specific treatment: it is that of money. Even minor issues to do with money can produce a lot of low-level stress in a marriage and, if there is a major financial problem, then it is capable of causing any number of explosive rows and sleepless nights. In some cases, financial problems can be a major factor in marriage breakdown. There is a vast amount that could be written about money matters and it is well worthwhile accumulating good financial advice, whether from your bank (who should have helpful leaflets on financial management), from books or from articles. It is also worth making the point that the issues here are not just about money; they are about how a marriage functions and how decisions are made. Decisions here have to be made jointly: if both parties do not make them, they can become a major source of friction in a marriage.

I would like, here, to give a few items of advice:

- In the initial stages of a marriage, be very cautious indeed about expenditure. It takes time to find out how much being married costs and to learn how to manage shared finances. To start married life in debt is an unhealthy beginning.
- Get the right attitude to finance. The old adage that money 'doesn't buy happiness' is actually true. Money claims to offer contentment and peace of mind but rarely, if ever, gives it and it is questionable whether marriages where there is wealth are any happier than those where there is only a limited amount of money. Nevertheless, beware the fantasy that poverty is great – it isn't. The following Old Testament prayer is a wise one. 'O God, I beg two favours from you before I die. First, help me never to tell a lie. Second, give me neither poverty nor riches! Give me just enough to satisfy my needs. For if I grow rich, I may deny you and say, "Who is the Lord?" And if I am too poor, I may steal and thus insult God's holy name' (Prov. 30:7–9).

> *Inquirer at funeral of millionaire, to accountant: 'How much did he leave behind?' Accountant: 'All of it.'*

- Linked with the right attitude to finance is the necessity of setting sensible goals. Don't be over-ambitious for things. After all, however much you get there will always be someone else with more. Relax! There is a lot more to life than possessions.

- Keep account of your money. It is tempting when things get rough to close your eyes and hope that the problem will go away. It won't. Keep track of your finances. It is a good idea to get monthly bank statements and to go over them together, itemising how much is being spent.

- Budget! Decide what you can afford, leave some slack for emergencies, and stay within those limits. In Charles Dickens' book *David Copperfield*, Mr Micawber said, 'Annual income twenty pounds, annual expenditure £19 19s 6d, result

> *People who think money can do anything may very well be suspected of doing anything for money.*
>
> **Mary Pettibone Poole**

happiness. Annual income twenty pounds, annual expenditure £20 0s 6d, result misery.' Despite inflation and decimalisation, Mr Micawber's rule still applies.

- Examine where the money is going. It is foolishness to save pence each month by buying cheaper food, when the real problem is the hundreds of pounds that your new car is costing you.

- Be very cautious about purchasing anything of any significant cost on impulse. Read the small print (and then re-read it), do the sums and talk it through together. Ask whether you really need it, rather than merely want it. Then sleep on the decision before committing yourself.

- Beware of credit. These days it is far too easy to become over-extended on borrowed money. Consider credit for what it is: an unpaid bill that, one day, will have to be paid. Ideally, you ought to face the future with money in the bank, not debts.

- You shouldn't get into the habit of making yourself feel better by going shopping. 'Retail therapy' is not the answer to anyone's problems. Try to address the root cause of any unhappiness, rather than just throwing money at it.

- Don't just do something because everybody else does – be independent. So, for example, never change a car you are happy with just because your friends have a new one; never go on an expensive holiday just because everybody else is doing it; and never buy a larger house than you need just because of what others will think. Be independent and delight in being independent. One of the great things about being a Christian is the freedom that it gives you to ignore the pressures of the culture around you.

- Be wary of ambition. A perfectly reasonable desire to earn money and have a successful career can easily become twisted into a desperate hunger to earn more than you need. Spouse and children easily become the first casualties in this case.

- Try to build into your finances some sort of savings for 'a rainy day'. A sudden period of unemployment or an illness that prevents you from working can be bad enough, but if there are already debts that need paying, then the financial repercussions of something like unemployment or an illness can be made very much worse. That pain can be reduced if there is a bit of surplus money in the account.

A person's treatment of money is the most decisive test of their character, how they make it and how they spend it.

James Moffatt

- Beware of wishfully thinking that 'something will

turn up'. This is the financial equivalent of Rosy Romanticism: the belief that you will get a salary increase, that the Inland Revenue will pay you tax back, or your rich aunt will die and leave you everything. Almost always, the reality turns out to be something else: there is no increase, the Inland Revenue decides that you have underpaid tax and your aunt doesn't die (or, if she does, it all goes to charity). In many people's experience, the only 'something' that does turn up is another bill!

- Try to plan ahead, and when it looks as though you are heading for trouble, take financial advice promptly and well before your cheques bounce. In general, most banks will be sympathetic where there is a short-term financial crisis due to some unforeseen circumstance,

> *If money be not thy servant, it will be thy master. The covetous man cannot so properly be said to possess wealth, as that may be said to possess him.*
>
> **Francis Bacon**

and may be able to extend loan periods. But they prefer it if you see them at the first hint of trouble.

- Some people get themselves into trouble by borrowing from a new source to pay off an existing debt. And when that source needs paying off, then they have to borrow from a third source and so on. Each time, the interest and charges will rise. Keep clear of such things.

- Be very careful about blaming each other over financial problems. I'm sure you know the scenario: a couple look at a bad bank statement and the shouting begins, 'This mess is your fault!' 'No it's not, it's yours!' and so on. In this way, they let the hurt and anger about the financial problem become focused into the marriage and directed against each other. It is far better to avoid the 'blame game' by saying, 'Okay, we are in trouble. What do we do about it?'

- Avoid the temptation to be involved in dubious financial schemes. Such schemes range from getting a massive mortgage so that you can make money on property price rises, through to investing in morally questionable high-risk investments. Obviously, when the concern is over the morality of what is being done, a married couple must decide for themselves what is right. Yet putting such issues of right and wrong to one side, the fact is that, even when they work, such schemes rarely solve financial problems. The well-founded traditional wisdom is that money that arrives rapidly is likely to depart just as fast, and I suspect that this is because in such cases there is always the temptation to try to make even more. When such get-rich-quick schemes fail, they can often be catastrophic.

- It is a wise idea to make sure that you are covered by adequate pension schemes for the future. How far you choose to be covered by insurance is another decision that you have to make and which will reflect your own priorities.

- Finally, learn to give. The advice to give may seem to fly in the face of all sensible financial wisdom and to be something exclusively for those who believe in a God who is interested in how we use our money. But it is more than that: by giving, especially by giving so much that it hurts, what you are demonstrating is that money has no hold over you. Every serious act of giving helps destroy the temptation to worship money or possessions.

You get more than you give when you give more than you get.

Living as a new family

A fundamental point about a marriage is that the husband and wife are now united as one. As anything that affects a husband affects his wife and vice versa, the fundamental basis of a marriage is one of mutual support and assistance. Because of the unity that there is between a husband and a wife, there are two tasks in a marriage: the positive task of supporting each other and the negative task of defending each other. Both overlap with aspects of the psychological bonding.

Mutual support

A key part of loving your spouse is to want to build him or her up by encouragement and support. You believe in them – so let them know it. It is a wonderful thing where, through the encouragement of a spouse, someone is enabled to fulfil their dreams. So, for instance, a husband might encourage his wife to do a course of study that she has always wanted to do, or a wife may support her husband in taking up a new job. On a more day-to-day basis, the importance of regular mutual support in a marriage cannot be overestimated. A husband or wife may spend a day getting abuse or criticism at work, but should always be able to return home to find it a place where their spouse consoles, supports and encourages them. This domestic 'recharging of the batteries' ought to enable them to go out and face a hostile world the following day with a new vigour and confidence. During tough periods of life, a home can be like the corner of a boxing ring; a place where the bruised combatant returns to after each round in order to be patched up and sent out again.

In mutual support, listen sympathetically and respect-fully to your spouse and remember to give praise. We all need praise, but some people never hear it. Part of the job of a spouse should be to give praise whenever it's due: and sometimes, maybe even when it isn't. But avoid mounting your spouse on a pedestal – people can fall off pedestals and hurt themselves.

Mutual defence

In marriage, it should never be forgotten that the husband and wife are each part of a team and are both playing on the same side: they are allies (in fact, more than allies) and never ever enemies. When you think of yourself and your spouse, it should be as *us* rather than *me and them*. And as part of a team, your job is always to protect your marriage partner. For instance, I can think of very few occasions when it would be right for someone to say something critical about his or her spouse to someone else.[1] Because you are so united, to give such criticism would be to score an own goal anyway. Make it a point of honour to defend your spouse.

Such support has at least two benefits. One, the fact that you have someone who is automatically on your side will give anyone confidence. And two, by presenting a united front, the development of any crack of criticism in a marriage is less likely. As such cracks are places where affairs can gain a foothold, this is important. So, if a husband has a rule of never criticising his wife in the presence of others, he is unlikely to have one of those dangerous conversations that begins 'My wife doesn't understand me . . .' And, of course, the same applies to a wife.

Equally, never add your criticism to that of the outside world. For instance, if you want to tackle your spouse

---

[1] I can think of two exceptions to this rule: a) where there has been abuse or ill treatment – the principle of mutual support should never be used to cover up something that is wrong and b) where someone is asking for help in handling a difficult marriage situation.

over something one day and it turns out that they have had a problem at work, then leave your own issue for another time. Try to stand alongside your spouse so that any attack is seen as *Praise does wonders for the sense of hearing.* being directed on both of you, rather than on them alone. Sticking by your spouse and supporting them when they are under pressure or attack, is a good way of cementing a marriage.

Now I am aware that this leaves all sorts of hard questions unanswered. What do you do when the criticism of your spouse is fair? What do you do when he or she really is in the wrong job or has made a mistake? There are no easy answers here, but any solution must involve tenderness and love. The rule Jesus gave of 'do for others what you would like them to do for you' (Mt. 7:12) is particularly applicable here. After all, as your spouse is inextricably linked with you, when you deal with them you are dealing with yourself.

Children

No mention of the social dimension in marriage would be even remotely complete without mention of children. However, this is not a book on parenting and so I want to be brief in my comments in this area.

Having a family is like having a bowling alley installed in your brain.

Martin Mull

You need to remember that although children are a tremendous joy and blessing, they do have an enormous impact in every area of a marriage and, in fact, change the whole dynamic of how a marriage functions. It is fallacy to assume that because babies are physically little, their impact is correspondingly small. It isn't – everything changes. Certainly, the arrival of a baby[2] needs careful consideration. One of the good things in the current age is the ability, through contraception, to plan families. Another is the upward extension of the age of normal childbearing. Until relatively recently, there was a good deal of pressure on a married couple to have children before the wife entered her thirties, but this pressure has now been lifted considerably. The combined result of these two developments is that, for most couples, marriage does not automatically mean starting a brief countdown to pregnancy. As the arrival of a child in the formative stages of a marriage can add a great deal of extra strain, this delay is to be welcomed.

In fact, I think that married couples need to give careful thought to why they want to have children. Many of the reasons why people have children are, frankly, inadequate. Let me list some reasons for having children that are, in my opinion, defective and, in some cases, much worse than that.

- 'A marriage is incomplete without children.'
- 'Children will prove that I am virile or fertile.'
- 'My mother or father want grandchildren.'
- 'Children will cement my marriage.'
- 'Children will give my life meaning.'
- 'My friends have them.'

Of course, there are bad reasons for not wanting children as well. Let me suggest the following reasons as a pretty inadequate basis for *not* wanting children.

- 'Children will destroy our lifestyle.'

---

[2] The common expression 'starting a family' should be avoided as a husband and wife on their own are still a family.

- 'Children cost too much.'
- 'Children won't go with the décor.'
- 'We'll have to get rid of the sports car.'
- 'It will annoy your mother.'
- 'Nappies.'

The fact is that, although a delight and a joy, children are an awesome responsibility and I can well understand the attitude of any couple who felt that they were not up to the demands of rearing children. Ironically, the reality is that such thoughtful and concerned people would, no doubt, actually make better parents than many people who just seem to have children without thinking about it at all. Children, like marriage itself, are great, but like marriage, they are not a venture to be embarked upon lightly. Having children should never be an impulse decision.

It is one thing to decide that you want children; it is another thing to have them. Even with the great advantages in reproductive medicine, the appearance of children cannot be guaranteed. Childlessness is a serious problem, where the parties involved may feel hurt, guilty or inadequate. Dealing with the complex medical, ethical and psychological issues of childlessness and its possible remedies (such as IVF, adoption and surrogacy) is beyond the scope of this book. But all couples would do well to remember that childlessness is a major and often traumatic issue. Handled well, childlessness is a crisis that can unite a couple and strengthen the bonds between them; handled badly, it can quickly tear the heart out of a marriage.

The social dimension: conclusion

Whether the couple are aware of it or not, every marriage represents the creation of something fresh and new in social terms: a new family, a fresh start. To a greater extent than they imagine, most newly-wed couples have a blank slate upon which they can create whatever they want.

If this is you, I want to encourage you to take the initiative. Look at the backgrounds and traditions that you have both come from and draw out of them those things that are good and that you value. Agree to hold to them in your marriage. Where the past gives no guidance, or sometimes, even where it does, make up your own traditions together. Of course, in doing this you will have to decide what you hold dear and what you value. To take just one issue, think of Christmas. How you decide to celebrate it, with churchgoing, partying or food, and who you celebrate it with, will reflect what you think it is all about. These issues have to be faced at some time or another and they may as well be faced at the start of a marriage.

The Psychological Dimension of Marriage

The third area of bonding between a man and a woman in a marriage is in the realm of the psychological. That cold technical term 'psychological' in fact covers the whole vast world of companionship, conversation and communication. It also covers those areas of problem solving and conflict resolution, but these are so important that I want to treat them separately in the next chapter. As with the other areas of marriage, the psychological dimension is so enormous that all I can do here is point out some of the main highlights in it and to map out some of the major hazards.

Often the difference between a successful marriage and a mediocre one consists of leaving about three or four things a day unsaid.

Harlin Miller

Within the psychological dimension, two distinct areas can be recognised. One is the region of those general principles that apply to every marriage and the other those specific issues and problems that are different in every marriage.

General principles

One of the curiosities of marriage is that many people fail to appreciate that there is a psychological dimension. In fact, some people tend to view their spouses as mirror images of themselves and to rationalise any differences as quirks or aberrations. So, he is aghast that she finds the idea of watching a football match unthinkable, and she is amazed that he never notices that she has had her hair done. To overlook the psychological dimension of a marriage is not a good idea. Mind you, the other extreme of regularly treating your spouse to a full-scale spell of Freudian psychoanalysis is not very smart either.

The following general principles apply, I think, to every marriage:

- Make a point in your thinking of dwelling on your spouse's good points and of skimming quickly over his or her bad points. This is not being un-realistic – you are not denying that failings exist – it is making an effort to overcome the inevitable tendency to

  > *I now perceive one immense omission in my psychology – the deepest principle of Human Nature is the craving to be appreciated.*
  >
  > **William James**

  let the bad outweigh the good. In particular, don't waste time mentally rehearsing what your spouse isn't, especially if it is something – such as intellect or appearance – that can't be changed.

- Major on appreciation rather than criticism. There is an old adage that there should be three items of praise for every one of criticism, and I'd treat that as a minimum. Remember that appreciation does not automatically occur; you need to make a positive decision to praise.

- Giving criticism is always hard, especially if your spouse is sensitive. If possible, try other strategies first. One classic alternative is to engage in what is called 'positive reinforcement' by praising them when they do the right thing. So, for instance, if you have been trying to get him to do more housework, compliment him when, voluntarily, he does the washing-up. Of course, such techniques don't always work and sometimes people don't take the hint, but the principle is a good one. Sometimes the carrot of praise is more effective than the stick of criticism. It certainly leaves fewer bruises.

> *A man had received intensive marriage counselling. He reported to his wife 'Darling, I got a wonderful insight. I learned that I'm constantly talking about myself. This has to change! You talk about me.'*
>
> **Herbert Strear**

- Aim for contentment in your relationship. In our modern frantic world we major on excitement, but the reality is that while we like excitement as a spice of life, the main psychological nutrients for existence are found in contentment. You know, the purring noise that you get when you stroke a well-fed cat on a warm rug? What you need to seek in your marriage is the inaudible, but still recognisable, human equivalent.

- Do what you can to boost your spouse's self-esteem. In an impersonal age, it is easy for people to feel downtrodden and devalued and it is vital that a marriage is a place where they are given a sense of value and worth. So, for instance, never take your spouse for granted. Talk to them about how they spend their day at work or at home. Be interested. When you face a family problem or issue, ask for your spouse's advice or opinion, even if you already know the answer. It affirms them and makes them feel wanted. And do remember to take their answer seriously, after all, they might just be right! Even during disagreements, show your spouse respect. Another side of this is to try to avoid surprising your spouse by making sudden arbitrary and unilateral decisions. To do that can be interpreted as saying, in effect, 'I don't need your input into decision-making.' If you are unconvinced about the importance of self-esteem, it is worth remembering that a major reason why men and women get involved in an extra-marital affair is because they feel undervalued at home and have found someone else who is interested in them and who takes them seriously.

- Be willing to forgive and to be a forgiver. I will talk about the hard, but necessary skill of forgiveness later, but here I want to point out that, with respect to forgiveness and bonds, there are three sorts of people. There are those who forgive readily and who, as a consequence, easily build bonds in their marriages; there are the reluctant forgivers who prevent marriage bonds from forming; and there are the criticisers and accusers, who, all too easily, break already existing bonds.

- Be a good listener. It has been widely noted that men fail in this area. While men talk about their problems in order to get an answer, women tend to talk about their problems in order to get sympathy. And when women do talk about their problems, men tend to assume that what they want is answers and

My wife said I never listen to her. At least I think that's what she said.

promptly (and frustratingly) leap in with helpful suggestions or lectures. In all probability, the woman already knows the answer; she is really looking for empathy. In fact, the most appropriate answer may be to say nothing and give her a hug.

- Although I view children as a gift from God, there is no doubt that they pose a number of specific threats in the psychological dimension of any marriage. Let me mention two in particular. The first is that when a baby arrives, husbands can feel alienated or rejected, as their wife suddenly switches into 'mother mode' and makes the new family member the focus of her attention. The second is that at a very early age, children learn to play one parent off against another in order to get their own way. The result can be to create tension between the husband and wife. A good operating rule is always to back each other up in front of the children, after all, no parent likes being overruled in front of their own child. Where there are disagreements, discuss them in private later.

- Encourage the right use of humour. I believe that humour is a God-given mechanism for defusing crises and easing diffi-culties and that for you to be able to laugh at yourself is an extra-

Our five senses are incomplete without the sixth – a sense of humour.

ordinarily valuable gift. Nevertheless, humour can be abused. Remember that even if an insult is wrapped up with a joke and a smile, it remains an insult and may be taken as one.

• Irrespective of the importance of sex and romantic love in a marriage, make it your aim to be your spouse's best friend. Ask yourself whether, if there was a crisis (excluding, of course, one that involved you), would you be the first person that your spouse turned to? If not, then you need to do some work in the area of psychological bonding.

Specific issues

There is more to handling the psychological dimension of marriage than just following general principles. Every marriage is different, and in each marriage there will be specific issues in the area of the psychological dimension that need to be dealt with.

The first step towards understanding your spouse's special needs is to realise that they see things differently. To understand how they do this requires tuning in to your spouse's mental wavelength and trying to see things as they see them. For instance, imagine that one summer's evening, a husband and wife come back to their home a few minutes apart. It would be easy to assume that both of them observe the same things, after all, the reality is the same. But she may notice that the sprawling rose bush in the garden needs trimming, that there is dirt on the carpet, that the flowers on the mantelpiece have faded and that the curtains need straightening. He may see none of

Spread love everywhere you go: first of all in your own house. Give love to your children, to your wife or husband, to a next-door neighbour . . . Let no one ever come to you without leaving better and happier. Be the living expression of God's kindness: kindness in your face, kindness in your eyes, kindness in your smile, kindness in your warm greeting.

Mother Theresa

those things, but may instead see that the gutter is sagging, that the front door needs repainting and notice from the purr of the video recorder that it is taping the cricket. Their feelings may differ too: she may feel exhilaration at being back in the security of her home; he may feel unease at all the tasks that he feels he needs to do. Perceptions differ.

In all long-term, quality marriages, the husband and the wife have learned to understand each other deeply. Sometimes they may not be able to say exactly how or why they understand each other; they only know that they do. So she can tell when he is getting bored with shopping and he knows when, for all her polite approval, she doesn't really want to go out for a meal. Both of them have learned to tune into each other's wavelength and to pick up the subtlest non-verbal signals. The secret to understanding these differences is, of course, good communication (and time), but to really map how your spouse operates psychologically may need more than routine communication. Assume that they see things differently to you and ask them what they like (or dislike) about something familiar (perhaps your home, your community, a film or a book). Or get them to talk about their childhood or schooling. And as you listen to their answers, try to draw out why they give the answers that they do.

Part of the mutual exploration that a husband and wife undertake in marriage involves the progressive understanding of the most intimate parts of each other's minds. As, in marriage, there is an uncovering of the partners' physical body in sex, so there should also be a parallel uncovering of their psychological being.

> *Husbands are awkward things to deal with; even keeping them in hot water will not make them tender.*
>
> **Mary Buckley**

In the best marriages the husband and wife know and share each other's deepest hopes and fears. Such an intimacy is something that is not lightly achieved: it takes time, patience, love and trust.

Yet to simply gain an understanding of your spouse is not enough. After all, they are not simply some laboratory specimen. What is learned must be applied in helping, strengthening and supporting them. There are two great principles here: negatively, never use your understanding for harm and positively, always use it for your spouse's good. Let's deal with each of these in turn.

Never use your understanding for harm

In this psychological dimension of a marriage, some things are to be avoided at all costs. Any couple who have been married for more than a few months have the knowledge to inflict enormous psychological injuries on each other. Each will know the other's soft spots, unresolved hurts and unhealed wounds, and such knowledge can be abused. For instance, he may know that she has always deeply doubted her ability to be a good mother, and so for him to say in the midst of a row, 'Your fears were true, you are a lousy mother!' is to plunge the knife – and twist it – where it will do most harm. And if he has profound doubts over his sexual ability, for her to shout at him, 'And actually you are pathetic in bed!' is to kick him where it really hurts. Of such things are

> *He who slings mud generally loses ground.*
> **Adlai Stevenson**

divorces (and domestic murders) made. Avoid at all costs. Even to abuse knowledge on a less severe scale can have negative consequences. When one partner in a marriage realises that there is the possibility that any revelations they give may be used against them, they will limit any psychological intimacy in self-defence, and a protective barrier is formed. Once trust is abused, any psychological intimacy will soon be lost.

More subtle misuses are possible. With the knowledge they have learned, a husband or wife can, if they are so minded, manipulate their partner. For example, a wife may realise that because her husband is concerned about ageing, she can get him to do almost anything about the house with the faintest hint that possibly he may 'no longer be up to it'. Or a husband may decide that because his wife is worried about her ability to be an adequate spouse, he can play on this to get his own way in the marriage. This is manipulation: it is the stuff of comedies, but in real life it is rarely amusing. Such psychological manipulation or emotional blackmail is something that is the opposite of love and, for all sorts of reasons, is to be shunned.

> *Express appreciation for each other. Accepting each other makes a stable marriage. Appreciating each other, however, makes a sensational marriage.*
> **Bret Selby**

Another misuse is that of passing on either accidentally (bad) or deliberately (much worse) what you have learned about your spouse. Relationship issues are things that should be kept private and should be revealed to someone else *only* by mutual consent. Intimacy must have confidentiality or else it dies. You can have a public relationship with someone or a private and intimate relationship, but you cannot have both.

Always use your understanding for your spouse's good

While there may be wrong uses of what you know about your spouse, there are many right and good uses of such knowledge. At the start of a marriage – and with regular reminders

> *Co-operation is spelled with two letters: WE.*

throughout – each party should resolve that they will do whatever they can to avoid hurting each other and to always build each other up. To do this is simply part of the teamwork of marriage.

Let me give some suggestions on how this sort of positive and healing use of psychological understanding can occur:

- She finds out that her husband has a problem with low self-esteem because of a psychologically abusive father. As a result, she makes praising him a major priority whenever appropriate.
- He learns that his wife's piano playing is not just a hobby, it is her way of unwinding, de-stressing and expressing the things she can't say with words. Although unmusical himself, he makes sure that her piano-playing time is uninterrupted.
- She discovers that because of his background he is a perfectionist with a desperate need to succeed and has a chronic fear of failure. Over time, she encourages him to take a more relaxed attitude to things and even to laugh at his disappointments.
- He realises that her way of handling her work stresses is for her to be silent at home. With that knowledge, he doesn't try to pressure her for immediate explanations of what is wrong. He just silently comforts her by giving her a hug.
- She realises that her husband is sensitive about being taken for granted because he grew up surrounded and over-shadowed by numerous brothers. Because of this, she goes out of her way to show her appreciation.

> *Marriage is a continuous process and not a static condition. It is a plant and not a piece of furniture.*
> **Harold Nicholson**

- He finds out that at school she was teased painfully about her accent and is still sensitive about it. He goes out of his way to never ever mention it.
- Because he is having work troubles, she makes a point of letting him know that she's aware of the pressure he's under. She 'deliberately forgets' to remind him that he promised to repaint the kitchen.

The psychological dimension: conclusion

The breadth and depth of the issues here are enormous: self-esteem, guilt, shyness, stress and a hundred other things. Although the matters that make up the psychological dimension of marriage are invisible, it is in this area that a marriage can make the most dramatic changes in someone's life. A healthy and supportive marriage can take a shy, insecure person with any number of problems and, over time, turn them into a confident, mature and well-balanced person. Sadly though, the opposite can be true, and a bad marriage can do a great deal of psychological damage. Physical abuse within marriages does occur and is a terrible thing, but I suspect that the suffering which psychological abuse inflicts is both far greater and far more widespread. Get the psychological dimension even partly right and a marriage can be a place of psychological healing; get it wrong and a marriage can be a seething pit of almost unendurable torment.

The Spiritual Dimension of Marriage

There are several reasons for leaving the spiritual dimension of marriage until last, but not because it is the least important. Even if the spiritual dimension is not recognised or acknowledged it is still vital. In fact, it is not really a separate dimension, because it is something that runs through every area of life and affects everything we do. If the spiritual dimension is recognised in a marriage and its value shared, then it can be a tremendous influence for the good of a marriage.

But before I look at some of the areas where the spiritual dimension is especially important, I want to make two very important points about how we look at spiritual matters.

The first is that we all come from some position of faith. A Christian has faith that there is a God and an atheist has the faith that there is not a God. Even the agnostic has faith: they have the faith that the evidence for God is inadequate. Many other people hold strongly to the faith that 'it doesn't matter what you believe'. These are all positions of faith. I make no secret that my own faith is Christian, and whether or not you have a name for your faith, you do have one.

The second point is that because we all have a faith there is no neutral ground from which to look at spiritual matters. We all view things from the perspective of our own faith and, whether we are atheists or Christians, our beliefs colour our view of things. The idea that only the agnostic or the atheist can view matters of faith with a cold, neutral and unbiased eye is nonsense. They have their own biases. And because we all hold to some sort of faith, there ought to be no room for any view that treats religion as if it was the result of some sort of peculiar or substandard mental thinking. With these warnings in mind, let's look at some of the different areas of married life that the spiritual dimension makes a direct and obvious impact on.

Values

In any marriage there has to be some shared moral values; some common beliefs in what is right or wrong. If there is not, the whole marriage structure will come unstuck pretty quickly. For instance, what happens when he believes that fiddling taxes is legitimate and she considers it wrong? Or one partner considers that lying is acceptable?

But where do values come from? I am taking for granted in this book that, for example, gentleness is better than violence, tolerance is better than hatred, love is better than anger, truth is better than lies, and that women and men should be treated as of equal worth. In doing this, I assume that most of my readers will recognise these values as ones that they can identify with. Yet such values, and many others that most of us hold dearly to, are not self-evident truths; they do not come imprinted on our brains, and they cannot be proved true by science. In fact, some of these values defy science. For instance, a recent survey suggested that primary school bullies are healthier and mentally stronger than their victims and that 'bullying may be good for you'. Yet no one would, I hope, defend bullying. The fact is (and for many people it is a rather disconcerting fact) that ultimately, effective values have to come from a spiritual source of some sort. But the problem is that many people have values that do not come directly from a spiritual source, but which have been acquired second-hand. For instance in Britain today, most people hold to the moral values of Christianity (such as honesty, truth, forgiveness, fairness and justice) without personally believing in Jesus. Yet, to hold to the moral values of any religion, particularly Christianity, without actually believing in it, is illogical. Furthermore, to hold onto the values of faith, but not the faith itself, is a strategy with a built-in expiry date: you are hoping to eat fruit from a tree that you are allowing to die.

In short, all marriages need values and the only source of such values is a set of beliefs that we could label as 'spiritual'. And if you like what we can term 'Christian values' then you need to realise that they won't last if transplanted out of the soil of Christian belief. Where there are shared values, then there is a strong foundation for marriage. Both parties believe in the same things; they are 'playing the game by the same rules' – only it is far more serious than any game.

Purpose

Spiritual input is also vital in giving a marriage purpose. The question of the purpose of marriage (or life generally) is such a hard one that many people today dodge it with a shrug of their shoulders or an embarrassed laugh. But what is a marriage for: are a married couple simply child producers; joint consumers; live-in lovers who share a name and bills? Or are they something more? Without a sense of purpose or a goal, a marriage can soon become little more than a series of exercises in survival.

Not only is the spiritual dimension the only source for values, but it is also the only source for purpose. Without God, the only reason for our existence seems to be to transmit our genes on to the next generation. And that seems to me to be a pretty pointless basis for living. For the Christian, marriage, like life itself, has purpose and meaning. It is a partnership of mutual support between a husband and a wife so that they can, together, serve God in this world. There may be challenges, discouragements and difficulties, but for the Christian couple there ought never to be a lack of meaning and purpose in their relationship.

Strength

If you haven't yet realised that a marriage requires a great deal of work, I can only assume that you are either not married or you are reading this on your honeymoon. A marriage makes tremendous demands, and sometimes these can be more than any individual can bear. Let me list some examples:

- Your patience with your squabbling children is exhausted and you want to walk out.
- You have had a lousy day at work, you feel like you are catching flu and yet your spouse has planned a meal out that can't be cancelled.
- You were psychologically bullied by your father, and now, years later, you realise to your utter horror, that you are treating your children the same way.
- Your spouse has just been fired from their job.
- Out of the blue, your spouse has admitted an affair and is now asking for your forgiveness.

In each case there is a genuine temptation to snap, lash out, collapse in despair or pack your bags and flee. It is in circumstances like these that people find that they need to draw on some external source of strength. For the Christian, God can become a source of strength at such times. Certainly, the experience of Christians over the ages is that they have felt enabled to draw upon God's peace, power and presence through the Holy Spirit in order to overcome or endure problems. And the idea that God himself is concerned about your marriage is something that is enormously encouraging. The way the spiritual dimension provides power is not just a personal and individualistic matter, there is a genuine benefit when both partners in a marriage can pray together about an issue. To say that 'the family that prays together, stays together' may be something of a cosy cliché, but there is more truth in it than many people realise.

Hope

The last area where the spiritual dimension is vital is the issue of hope. Sooner or later, a shadow falls over even the best marriages. In one marriage, the specialist confirms that there is no hope that the couple can have the children of their own that they always longed for. In another, the son on whom their hopes rested is awaiting trial on serious criminal charges. And in yet another, chronic ill health has turned a dream marriage into a long and painful ordeal. But we don't have to think of hypothetical situations, because the dark cloud of death edges nearer to all of us every day. The truth is that if there is no hope of life beyond death, even the greatest marriages are, ultimately, tragedies. But for the Christian, with their belief that Jesus will one day raise them from death to eternal life, death is not the final end. It is, in fact, merely the beginning of our real lives.[3] The practical importance of this aspect of spiritual hope is enormous. The Christian knows God as their heavenly Father and can face the future not with fear, but with expectant joy.

---

[3] I should mention that Jesus plainly teaches that the married state does not continue in heaven (Mt. 22:30). While we may know and recognize each other there, we will clearly not relate to each other in the exclusive paired and sexual relationships that we have here. We do not know what relationships in eternity will be like. In speculating on such matters, we are in a similar position to a tadpole trying to imagine what it must be like to be a frog.

What if I have no spiritual faith?

Finally, let me say something to anybody reading this who has no formal religious faith. Perhaps you are married to someone who has come to faith and you are puzzled and bewildered by what you see happening.

If you do not have a Christian faith and are married to someone who has, let me urge you first of all to be sympathetic and understanding. For one thing, as I pointed out earlier, we all have faith in something, so the gap between you both may not be as large as you think. For another, don't think that the Christian believer doesn't understand anything of your frustration. You may find the religious point of view incomprehensible, but as a Christian I can say that I see the inability of the atheist to see the Christian point of view profoundly frustrating as well. Let me share an illustration that may help. You must have seen one of those images made up of a vast number of apparently random dots that, when you stare at them for long enough in the right way, suddenly become striking 3-D images.[4] Now some people can see the images, while others, despite their best efforts, can't. The result is that those people who can see the image don't understand how anyone can't see it, while those that can't see it protest loudly that the whole thing is obviously only a random pattern of dots. Now I think that this is a good illustration of the situation with regard to the Christian faith: in what one person can only see as the self-evidently random noise of the universe, another sees, as large as life, a clear image of God. To the 'non-believer' this illustration is a reminder that there may be more than one level of meaning to something. To the

---

[4] The technical (but little used) term for such images is a Single-Image Random-Dot Stereogram (SIRDS).

'believer' this illustration makes the point that the basis of your faith may not be as obvious to others as it is to you.

Finally, if you are someone who has closed the door to the 'spiritual world' can I urge you to consider re-opening it? Now, as a Christian, I cannot endorse all religious or spiritual beliefs: not all that is 'spiritual' is good or true and some spiritual things are harmful and false. Nevertheless, the first step to finding God is to open your eyes to the possibility that he is there to be found. A widespread pattern is that people think about religious or spiritual matters in their teens or early twenties (perhaps while they are students) but, even if the issues raised then are unresolved, they end up putting them to one side while they deal with the more pressing matters of life such as marriages and mortgages. As time goes on, the great question of God is never re-addressed and the matter becomes effectively closed. Yet the enormous undertaking of marriage, let alone parenting, raises questions. Why continue generations? What do we tell our children: about God; about what happens when we die; about right and wrong? How do you handle ageing and the onset of fading powers? Such questions can, and should, provide an enormous stimulus to review the issue of faith and the meaning of life.

The spiritual dimension: conclusion

Not only does the spiritual dimension exist in a marriage, but it is also important. A shared faith, common values, a belief that God cares for your marriage and a knowledge of something of his presence and power in your daily life can make an enormous difference to a marriage. It is hardly surprising that a psychological study showed that couples who joined in religious activities and who viewed their marriage as having spiritual importance, showed more marital satisfaction, had less frequent marital conflict, and resolved disagreements more successfully.[5]

There is a lot more that I would like to say on the spiritual side of marriage, but this is a book on marriage by a Christian and not a book on Christianity. If you want to pursue these matters further, the Appendix lists some of my other books, which you may find helpful.

[5] Reference: A. Mahoney, K.I. Pargament, T. Jewell, A.B. Swank, E. Scott, E. Emery, M. Rye, 'Marriage and the Spiritual Realm: The Role of Proximal and Distal Religious Constructs in Marital Functioning'. *Journal of Family Psychology* 1999, 13(3): 321–338.

PART TWO

Defending Marriage

Chapter 4

Resolving Conflicts

'Gordon,' Angela said, walking into the lounge with a letter in her hand. 'I'm just looking at the bank statement. Have you got a moment?'

With a twinge of foreboding, Gordon looked up from watching the television. 'Of course,' he said.

Angela frowned. 'It's this item. £195, Elliots, on 14 May. What's that?'

Gordon hesitated for a second. 'That? Oh, that . . . That would be the new car CD-radio.' He looked back at the television screen. At the end of a long day, he really didn't want to discuss the matter.

'That much! That's two hundred pounds!' There was irritation in her voice. 'We were supposed to be paying off the overdraft.'

'I told you about it,' Gordon protested.

'You never told me it was that much.'

'Didn't I? Well, I'm sorry.'

'It's too much. It's a major purchase.'

Gordon waited for a moment before answering. 'Look, it was a bargain. I sit in that car for over two hours a day. It keeps me sane. And you said it sounded nice.'

'You hadn't told me the price.' Angela shook her head angrily. 'It's not fair, Gordon.'

'What's not fair?'

'It's happened again. You bought that digital camera in the spring. In just the same way.' She angrily reached for the remote control and switched off the television.

'Hey, I was watching that!' Gordon was aware of a mounting anger.

'Tough. We have joint finances. We agreed.'

'Look,' Gordon said, aware of the tension in his voice. 'I'm sorry I overspent. Right?'

'No.' Angela threw the bank statement down angrily and put her hands on her hips. 'It's not "right". I work to try to save money and you do this!'

'Look woman, stop making it out to be such a big deal. You buy things without asking me. Our financial mess is as much your fault as mine. You wanted that holiday.'

There was a snort of angry disbelief. 'Huh! Oh, that's so typical of you Gordon. That's just so typical. Blame me. You always do that. Whenever I have a problem with you, you turn it around so that I become the one who is responsible.' He knew she was close to tears. 'Well, I've had enough,' Angela said suddenly, 'I wonder why I bother.'

Then she turned on her heel and stormed out, slamming the door behind her.

'And you aren't the only one either!' He shouted as he heard her footsteps go heavily upstairs.

With a sigh, Gordon sat back in his chair and picked up the remote control. His finger hanging over the 'on' button, he paused. Angry rows happened in every marriage, he decided: his was no different. He comforted himself with the idea that rows were like thunderstorms. They just blew up and there was nothing you could do about them except let them pass over you. They were, he concluded with a shake of his head, just a fact of life.

He switched the television back on.

Introduction

Is Gordon right? Are marriage conflicts just a fact of life? And do they just pass over? I suspect most of us realise that, while conflicts may occur, they can often be avoided, and that if they do occur, there are good and bad ways of handling them. This chapter covers marriage conflicts and how to resolve them.

Before I deal with conflicts, I want to make a distinction between problems and conflicts because, although related, they are actually separate things. I think a problem in a marriage is simply any issue or difficulty that needs solving or sorting out. Problems in marriage, as in life, are inevitable. But problems do not become more than that, as long as they are solved without anger, confrontation or strong disagreement. Conflicts occur where the problem has brought about a heated argument, a row or an angry silence. Conflicts are problems that have become infected.

While most of this chapter is devoted to looking at conflict, I want to make some comments on problems first.

Dealing with Problems

Every marriage has problems, and some have them on an almost daily basis. In some respects, they are just the bumps and hollows on

One of the nice things about problems is that a good many of them do not exist except in our imagination.

Steve Allen

the road of married life. Nevertheless, the way you deal with them is important for several reasons.

- Problems can grow or accumulate so that they

weaken or ruin a marriage. So, for example, a husband's habit of not tidying up may not be that serious if it is limited to the bedroom and occurs only sporadically. But if it spreads so that his wife feels that she spends her life tidying up after him, then it may become a major stress factor in the relationship. Over the years, the accumulation of a thousand small and petty problems can erode a marriage until it falls apart. To destroy a building by letting woodworm devastate it is not as spectacular as setting fire to it, but the outcome is the same.

- Problems may also indicate the issues over which the big conflicts will emerge. Major crises rarely come out of the blue, there is normally a history. If you asked a geologist where in a particular region a major earthquake was likely to occur, they would probably point out somewhere where lots of little and harmless earth tremors had already occurred. Similarly, problems in marriages tend to map out the fault lines along which the relationship could, in theory, pull itself apart. So in a marriage where there have been endless awkward moments over the way he imposes his will on her in little things, it may not be surprising if, one day, a major crisis blows up because he refuses to agree to her changing her job.

- Problems may be the flashpoints over which conflicts occur. So a problem occurs and then, either because it is mishandled or because other issues are dragged in, it rapidly escalates into a full-blown conflict.

- How problems are handled sets the pattern for how the big crises are handled. It may seem silly to link a trivial problem over who does the washing-up with a marriage-shaking crisis over whether to move house, yet the way that minor problems are or are not resolved may define the way that conflicts are dealt with. So, if, when he tackles her over some minor issue, she refuses to discuss the matter, but just shrugs her shoulders

When a man and woman marry they become one. The trouble starts when they try to decide which one.

and walks away, it will be no surprise if, when faced with a serious conflict, she does the same thing.

It is for these reasons that minor problems should not be overlooked. When they arise, seek to handle them as well as you can. Many of the strategies and principles I offer for handling conflicts can be employed to solve problems. In this way, you can use these problems as the training ground for resolving future conflicts.

Understanding, Avoiding and Preparing for Conflict

In the next section, I want to present ten principles for handling conflict. But before I do, I want to discuss a number of issues relating to conflict that we need to know about first.

a) Understand how conflicts develop

In order to learn to avoid or minimise conflict, it is useful to understand how conflicts occur. Conflicts do not normally appear in an instant: like living creatures, they grow and develop. In a marriage, conflicts tend to develop through four well-marked stages that we can call Challenge, Complaint, Criticism and Contempt. To illustrate these stages, let's watch what happens when, one day, when it's his turn to do the cooking, Barry serves up spaghetti bolognese for his wife Lynda. It's very fine spaghetti bolognese really: the problem is that it's the third time he's made it in the last fortnight. I'll let you imagine Barry's responses, because it's Lynda's that we want to watch.

1. *Challenge* is where one partner in a marriage raises an issue in such a way as to make it plain that they are unhappy about it. Faced with her plate of *Bolognese á la Barry* Lynda says in a quiet, but unmistakable tone, 'Bolognese again?' In theory, this could just be a neutral statement of facts. But it isn't. Lynda is making a challenge, expressing in a general way her unhappiness and dissatisfaction.

2. *Complaint* is the next stage. With complaint the challenge is now deepened and focused into a sharp and specific expression of dissatisfaction. So Lynda follows through by saying, 'I think we have bolognese too often.' There is now an accusing tone in her voice and although Barry might have overlooked her first comment, he can't overlook this.

3. With *Criticism*, there is a clear and unmistakable accusation of wrongdoing. Now Lynda says, 'You always make bolognese.' The temperature has risen even more. Notice the use of the word 'you' – this time, it's personal. And 'always' is hardly a neutral word either: it implies that this is a recurrent problem and that poor Barry is a persistent offender.

4. Criticism can easily pass into *Contempt*. Here, accusation is not enough – there is now a scornful, dismissive and hurtful edge to what is said. So now Lynda says, 'I suppose you cook bolognese so much because you can't cook anything else!'

Contempt isn't the final stage in a conflict; it's just the

final predictable stage. Once you reach the contempt level of conflict, the temperature is so high that almost anything can happen next. In the next stage ('Catastrophe'? 'Conflagration?'), there will doubtless be more angry accusations and counter-accusations and the conflict may easily be broadened out to cover other areas of the marriage. And, in the case of our illustration, the bolognese may well end up on the floor.

I have listed these stages because they point out one of the main characteristics of conflict – its deadly ability to escalate. Unchecked or restrained, conflict soon spirals out of control as each new stage arouses an angry response. But recognising these conflict stages is helpful for two other reasons. First, it forewarns you of problems: when you are faced by a challenge you need to be aware that a criticism may already be brewing. Second, it should encourage you to act at the earliest stages of a conflict.

> *Anger is a momentary madness, so control your passion or it will control you.*
>
> **Horace (65–8 BC)**

Clearly, the easiest place to stop a conflict is at the beginning, before it has got much beyond the 'challenge' stage. A conflict evolving under its own ruthless logic is like a car parked at the top of a steep hill whose brakes have been let off. If you are going to stop it, it is best to do it before it builds up speed.

b) Be aware of different reactions in conflict situations

A complicating factor in handling conflicts is that different people react in different ways to conflict situations. I think you can identify at least five different types of personality.

There are those personality types that won't put up a fight at all. There are *Retreaters*, those people who, at the first hint of an argument, back off with an apology and refuse to fight. Then there are *Defenders*, people who, while they will not run away from conflict, are reluctant to fight back. Defenders are rather like hedgehogs, they just quietly curl up into a ball, stick their prickles out and hope that the conflict will end. Then there are three types of personality who will fight. *Aggressors* are those types who are always looking for a fight and are quite ready to have a row anywhere, at any time, over almost anything. If you are married to an aggressor then you have my sympathy. Finally, there are two groups of people who, while they don't tend to start fights, will retaliate. The *Rapid Retaliators* are those people who, at the first hint of an argument, hit back swiftly and without hesitation. Their motto is 'So you want a fight do you? Well take that!' The *Reluctant Retaliators* are those people who, at first, refuse to fight and either retreat a short way or take a defensive stand but who, when provoked, eventually explode and retaliate.

It is important to identify how your spouse handles conflicts and to adapt accordingly. To imagine that your spouse is a Retreater, when in fact they are really a Reluctant Retaliator can be a disastrous mistake.

One other complicating factor is that our family backgrounds play an important part in how we handle conflict situations. Think of Harry, whose parents used to have violent rows regularly. The bad news is that because he has been brought up to think that rows are an inevitable part of life's routine, Harry can be rather careless about trying to prevent them from happening. However, the good news is that he has learned the dynamics of rows and conflicts and is skilled at handling and surviving them. Naomi, however, is very different: she was fortunate enough to be brought up in a family where conflict was dealt with at such an early stage that she never even noticed its presence. The good news is that, as a result, she has high expectations that conflict will not occur in her own marriage. The bad news is that when conflict does happen, she is utterly thrown by it, thinks it's the end of the world and makes it all much worse by handling it very badly.

c) Identify the main stress areas

It is a great help to identify those areas in your marriage where problems and conflicts are likely to develop. The following are eight areas of married life where conflicts seem to occur most commonly:

- Work
- In-laws
- Children and babies
- Money
- Sex
- Housework
- Conflicting personal habits
- Ill health and ageing

I have dealt with the first five of these stress areas. Concerning the last three, I merely want to make the briefest of comments.

Housework is, I'm afraid to say, an issue that is very much a 'gender thing'. On the whole, men are capable of living at a much lower level of hygiene and cleanliness than women are. It is not uncommon for a husband to be totally baffled by why his wife insists on vacuuming the house when she did it only last week or cleaning the bathroom when it was done last month. I do not, of course, defend such male attitudes, I merely note them.

Conflicting personal habits include such things as

untidiness, unreliability or unpunctuality. What may have been an amusing personality trait during courtship has, over the years of marriage, become something that irritates to an extraordinary degree.

Illness and ageing is an enormous area, including such things as loss of looks, age and illness-related changes in lifestyle, and a whole spectrum of medical issues. Problems and conflicts here can often be caused by a failure of one or both parties in a marriage to come to terms with the effects of these factors. For instance, imagine a couple who are in their late fifties and who, every year, have a week's camping holiday. This year she is still keen, while he is less enthusiastic. He now realises that he no longer has the energy and enthusiasm for it that he once had. Some-how, the two of them have to face this issue with all its overtones of ageing and mortality.

Adam and Eve had an ideal marriage. He didn't have to hear about all the men she could have married and she didn't have to hear about how well his mother cooked.

There is a need in every marriage to recognise those areas that pose particular problems for you, your spouse or both of you. Where you can, avoid them. Where you have no option but to face them, seek to minimise their effects. And all the time, communicate your feelings about these issues to your partner.

d) Recognise the danger conflict poses to your marriage

Even the best marriages are fragile and vulnerable things. Most of the time, most of us recognise this and unconsciously create rules to protect the destruction of our marriages. So we keep our voices down, refrain from talking about hurtful matters and seek to calm issues rather than inflaming them. The problem with conflict, however, is that, in the heat of the argument, any such self-imposed regulations get trampled on. The result can all too easily be conflicts in which appalling and sometimes irreparable damage can be done. Because the rulebook is torn up, once a conflict starts no one can

Turn to each other, not on each other.

predict the way that it will end. Imagine, for instance, a couple having a furious row. Full of fury, he lets slip that he thinks that she has become fat. Deeply hurt, she retaliates that she is ashamed of the way he behaves in public and wishes that she had never married him. After such things have been said, how can you get back to where you were? A few harsh words can wreck many years of patient toleration.

In this context, it may be helpful to think of a marriage as being like two people walking together along a narrow cliffside path, just a few feet from where a crumbling edge overhangs a hundred-foot drop. Any struggle will involve them moving out towards that edge and a major conflict poses a real risk that they both may plunge to destruction. Even a minor struggle cannot be risked: it would be all too easy to step on some unstable patch of ground that would suddenly give way. The explanation of why, from 1945 onwards, the global superpowers never came to a direct major conflict with each other is very relevant here. The reason was that each side realised that even a limited conflict might escalate out of control into one where nuclear weapons were used and both were destroyed. The term for that bleak scenario was 'Mutually Assured Destruction' with its appropriate acronym of MAD. It is worth realising that in any marriage there is the potential for domestic MAD, and its existence should have the same effect. Think twice before allowing a conflict to escalate!

e) Work at conciliation

The antidote to conflict is conciliation: the renewing of trust or agreement between parties and the restoration of relationships. Even where conflict is inevitable, a conciliatory attitude can make things a lot easier.

Have a heart that never hardens, and a touch that never hurts.

Charles Dickens

To practice conciliation is to try to defuse a conflict. If you think of conflict as a step-by-step ascent up the ladder of Challenge, Complaint, Criticism and Contempt, then conciliation is the attempt to stop that process. In conciliation, you are trying to neutralise and disarm anger. Remember the illustration of Barry, Lynda and the spaghetti bolognese that I used earlier? Now suppose that instead of making the challenge of 'Bolognese again?' Lynda had switched into conciliatory mode. She might have instead said something along the lines of, 'You know I was wondering if we could have a change from bolognese? Perhaps I could make a risotto tomorrow?'

This may seem a minor change, but notice four things about it.

1. The language ('you know', 'was wondering', 'perhaps I could') is now gentle and non-threatening.
2. The tone of negative disapproval has been changed to one of positive suggestion.
3. Although the original challenge did not use the word 'you', it was implied, and the effect was accusatory. A much more neutral and non-threatening 'we' has now replaced it. Instead of being divisive, Lynda's comment is now uniting.
4. Finally, in the offer to 'make a risotto tomorrow'

there is the proposal of a 'sacrificial' alternative. There is a problem, Lynda is saying, but let me, not you, bear the cost of solving it.

So conciliation can be brought in right at the start of a conflict and can stop the cycle of conflict from ever beginning. But conciliation can be brought in even later. So even if Lynda had uttered her challenge of 'Spaghetti again?' Barry might still have been able to make a conciliatory answer by saying something along the lines of, 'Sorry, Lynda, I was going to do a curry but I forgot to get some rice,' or 'Oh, I'm sorry, I had completely forgotten that we'd had it so recently.' Now for Barry to say either of these things, or anything similar, might not be easy; he might easily appear foolish. But then conciliation is never easy, especially when you feel that you are being attacked, and the temptation is always to retaliate in a similar vein. Other issues exist when the challenge or the accusation is unfair. Then you may have to balance the desire for conciliation against the necessity of tackling issues that really do need dealing with.

f) Realise that some conflict is inevitable

Many (and possibly, most) marriage conflicts can be avoided. Some, however, cannot. A marriage is where two people from different backgrounds, with their different outlooks and personalities try to unite as a single social unit. It is inevitable, in this uniting process, that there will be

> *Marriage is like life in this –*
> *that it is a field of battle,*
> *and not a bed of roses.*
>
> **Robert Louis Stevenson**

some confrontation, some grinding of gears as the two lives intermesh. In fact, to have a conflict is not an indication of a failing marriage. Actually, if a marriage conflict is successfully negotiated and resolved (and lessons from it learned) then it will be something that has helped a marriage to grow. Ironically, conflict may be a sign of life. After all, there are marriages that are so dead that there is little to fight about and no energy to fight about it with – no one cares enough to fight.

In fact, not only can some conflicts not be avoided – some conflicts shouldn't be avoided. For instance, imagine a situation in which a husband is constantly discouraging and belittling the children. His wife may be reluctant to tackle him over the issue, because she knows that if she does it will mean certain conflict, but for her to stay silent would be very wrong. Carefully and, if she is a Christian, prayerfully, she should try to raise the matter with him in as non-confrontational a way as possible.

Make it a rule to avoid conflict unless it is absolutely necessary – but remember that sometimes there are worse things than conflict.

g) Understand the principles of forgiveness

Before we can talk about conflict resolution, we need to think about the subject of forgiveness: one of the most important tools in defusing conflicts. Forgiveness is important in resolving conflicts because it stops the momentum of a dispute.

> *Once a woman has forgiven her man, she must not reheat his sins for breakfast.*
>
> **Marlene Dietrich**

As we have seen, most conflicts are like snowballs going down a hill; after one push, the whole thing starts rolling with rapidly increasing size and speed. Forgiveness, however, absorbs the energy and stops the whole process dead.

But what is forgiveness and what does it mean to forgive? Although forgiveness used to be considered a major virtue in our culture, its value has been largely lost:

today, people prefer to 'get even' instead. Because of the confusion nowadays about what forgiveness is, I think it is

One pardons in the degree that one loves.
La Rochefoucald

important that we clear up what forgiveness really is and is not. The following points should be born in mind.

- Forgiveness is the process where barriers of hate or guilt between people are removed, so that a relationship without hostility can either be restored or created between them. The removal of these barriers can be likened to paying off a debt for someone or setting them free.
- Forgiveness is first and foremost a decision, not an emotion. Forgiveness is something you decide to do, whether you feel like it or not. So, although emotionally you may feel like punishing someone who has done you wrong, forgiveness involves the decision, as an act of the will, to let them off. In this respect, forgiveness is like love and can be considered as the first step of the process of love. One implication of this is that you can't ever say 'I love my spouse but I can't forgive them'. There can be no love without forgiveness.
- Forgiveness is not necessarily an instantaneous event: it may be a process that takes some time. People can and do forgive in an instant, but where there has been a major hurt it can take time, sometimes years, to achieve full forgiveness. Nevertheless, the important thing is to start down the road of forgiveness.
- Forgiveness does not mean ignoring justice. Sometimes people give the impression that forgiveness means turning a blind eye to what is right or wrong. This is not the case, but the reality is that forgiveness does mean overlooking one's personal anger or

*He that cannot forgive
others, breaks the bridge
over which he himself must
pass if he would ever reach
heaven; for everyone has
need to be forgiven.*

George Herbert

hatred. A husband may forgive his wife for throwing a plate at him, but that does not mean that he agrees that this is an acceptable way of expressing feelings in a marriage.

- Forgiveness does not necessarily mean forgetting. In fact, forgetting is frequently impossible. How, for instance, could a wife forget her husband's adultery? What forgiveness does mean is putting the matter to one side so that it is no longer a barrier in the relationship. And it does mean that from now on, the particular issue over which there has been forgiveness can no longer be brought up. It has been placed 'out of play'.

- Forgiveness is, ideally, one half of a two-part process; the one who is wrong offers repentance and the one who is wronged offers forgiveness. The equation is that forgiveness plus repentance produces healing. This, of course, raises the issue of what happens when the offending party is unrepentant. This is a hard question, but I think that even here, forgiveness should be offered. Someone has to start the process off and even an incomplete healing is better than none.

- Forgiveness may be costly. It can mean forgoing revenge and giving up your own rights. It may even be misinterpreted as the act of a weak person.

- Although forgiveness is costly, the alternative is usually even more expensive. If we fail to forgive we become locked in the past and can never progress beyond the offence that we will not forgive. By failing to forgive, we lay ourselves open to feeling hatred and to being poisoned by our own bitterness.

Finally, I have to mention that, for the Christian, forgiveness must be a major priority. Forgiveness is something that has been shown to us by God through the death of his son Jesus Christ on the cross. As the Apostle Paul says in the Bible, 'He is so rich in kindness that he purchased our freedom through the blood of his Son, and our sins are forgiven' (Eph. 1:7). But Christians ought not to be people who only receive forgiveness; as imitators of Christ, they are also to practice it. As Paul also points out later in the same letter, 'Be kind to each other, tender hearted, forgiving one another, just as God through Christ has forgiven you' (Eph. 4:32). Christians are to be people who are both forgiven and forgiving.

h) Setting rules for handling conflict

Talk to anyone in the fire brigade and they will say that the best way to fight fires is a) stop them from happening in the first place and b) have measures in place to deal with them if they do occur. The same advice can be offered in respect of marriage conflicts: try to prevent them, but also have strategies in place for handling and containing conflicts if they do occur. The idea is to have rules to ensure that there is a 'fair fight' and that neither combatant suffers lasting damage.

There is a widespread reluctance in a marriage to actually think about how conflicts are going to be handled. Some of that reluctance comes from the wondrously naive view that 'conflicts won't happen to us', and some of it, doubtless, from the idea that to prepare for conflict in marriage is somehow to invite it. Nevertheless, if there is going to be conflict in a marriage, and all the evidence suggests there will be, then it is surely better to have some rules in place to govern what happens.

Let me suggest the sort of rules that you should agree to:

- Agree that there must be no physical violence. I shouldn't really have to say this but it is important to agree that throwing things, slapping, etc is quite off limits. Agree, too, that it is impermissible to even threaten to use violence.

- Agree that there must be no verbal abuse. 'Sticks and stones can break my bones but calling names won't hurt me' is the old playground chant, but sadly, it is a false claim. In fact, verbal abuse can be worse than physical abuse. Broken bones can heal, but for many people, the wounds made by insults never heal. Agree that calling each other names and insulting each other is not acceptable. Treat each other with respect (at the very least).

- Agree that certain issues and topics will not be brought up when you argue. You might, for instance, agree not to bring in such sensitive things as previous mistakes, past relationships or in-laws. Each couple should have their own list of things that they have decided between them to declare off limits. Such a list of excluded topics cannot be completely unbreakable – after all, it might be your in-laws that are the problem.

- Agree limits to your conflicts. These limits may be of space or time. So, for instance, you may agree on a principle of never arguing in bed or the bedroom, or never arguing beyond a particular time. I will talk more about this later.

- Agree to never threaten to walk out or end the marriage. Irrespective of whether you have agreed that divorce is not an option: to say something like, 'Right, I've had enough; I'm leaving you!' is quite unacceptable. To do this is to give up discussion in favour of verbal bullying. By threatening to use the 'ultimate weapon', the stakes have been raised to a point where it is impossible to continue the debate any further.

- Agree not to start a conflict just whenever you feel like it. Commit yourselves to postponing your disagreements until you can meet and talk together privately. Of course, this should be at the earliest opportunity, rather than being delayed indefinitely, but arguments are best dealt with in something like one of those Problem Management Sessions that I talked about in Chapter 1.

- Agree to let each other speak. It is all too easy for the one partner in a marriage to dominate a discussion and even to refuse to let the other party have their say. Promise that you will both let each other make those points that need to be expressed.

- Agree to forgive each other promptly. You may need to consider forgiveness and what it means more carefully. Both of you need to remember that only forgiveness will stop a conflict running on and on.

You might think up other rules that you would want to bring in, but my advice is don't be too unrealistic or the whole idea of agreed rules may end up being thrown away. Finally, why not write them down and put them somewhere safe and accessible?

Ten Principles for Handling Marriage Conflict

Conflict, at some point, is inevitable in any marriage. But when it occurs, how do we handle it?

Nowadays 'Conflict Resolution', whether for marriages,

businesses or even nations, is a major area of the social sciences and there are all sorts of books, tapes and courses on the subject. Much of what is taught under the name of conflict resolution is excellent and helpful, and if you find yourself in a marriage where conflict seems to be permanently on the agenda, then you may find some of these resources useful. Let me, however, give three warnings.

First, because a marriage is very different from the workplace, 'industrial strength' conflict resolution techniques can be quite inappropriate in a domestic dispute. You are dealing with a far deeper, more intimate and delicate relationship than that of employer–employee!

Second, there is a danger that, in the intimacy of marriage, suddenly bringing in conflict resolution techniques can come over as artificial and clichéd. So if one party in a marriage dispute suddenly starts to trot out phrases such as 'we are both stakeholders in this', 'we need to seek consensus here' or even 'believe me, I feel your pain' it may make matters worse. It is far better to go beyond applying techniques in specific moments of crisis, to incorporating principles into your marriage on a permanent basis. Conflict resolution is less like a course of antibiotics to be suddenly swallowed when an infection breaks out, and more like a course of vitamins that are taken on a daily basis.

Third, some types of conflict resolution carry with them philosophical or religious undertones that need careful examination.

Nevertheless, there are a number of important principles that can be identified for handling marriage conflicts correctly. Let me suggest ten in particular.

1. Put the relationship first

If you are in a marriage conflict situation, your objective must never be to achieve a personal victory. Because you are united to your spouse, a defeat for them is a defeat for both of you. This radical perspective requires a new attitude to dealing with conflicts, your priority now is not victory but resolution. The term 'conflict resolution' is not just a trendy cliché; it makes an important point. With resolution, both sides win and the marriage wins.

If your working life revolves around winning arguments or clinching deals, the idea of seeking to resolve, rather than to win, may be a concept that you need to work at. In order to achieve that resolution, your own pride may have to suffer. The Christian emphasis on being humble and being prepared to suffer is one that is very helpful in marriage. To put the relationship first means that you have to be prepared to lose face in front of your spouse. But then if you can't bear to lose face in front of your spouse, you have a problem that needs addressing. Let me make one more suggestion here: never ever allow yourself to get in the frame of mind where you see your spouse as 'the enemy'. To take such a view is to invite an almost inevitable marriage disaster.

2. Try to understand

One of the many half-truths that float around in our language is the statement 'to understand is to forgive'. In fact, understanding and forgiveness are two quite separate things. Nevertheless, it is undeniable that it is easier to sympathise and, therefore, to forgive, if we can see the situation through the other person's eyes.

Understanding is particularly vital in a marital conflict, because the real issues may not always be what they seem to be. For example, imagine a domestic row that on the surface is all about whether to replace a sofa. The real issue of the conflict may actually be that one party feels that they are being marginalised in the domestic decision-making process, or that they believe that the money should be spent elsewhere. The conflict may even be an expression of something totally different, perhaps the fact that someone has had a bad day at work. But if this dispute is really about deeper issues, or even something else altogether, to resolve the issue of the sofa may be only a temporary or partial solution: the real root issue of the problem may not have been addressed.

In a marital conflict, understanding what is really going on can often be hindered by gender differences.

A man walked into a bookstore and asked the woman behind the counter, 'Have you got a book called, Man, the Master of Woman?' 'Try the fiction section,' said the woman.

Men and women tend to engage in conflict in quite different ways. In a row, a woman is likely to come out with a flood of words and emotions. A man, in contrast, will probably be much less emotional: he is likely to coolly challenge her logic, correct her inaccuracies, pick at the details and try to show how unreasonable she is. It is rather odd that, even after thousands of years of failure, men still naively hold onto the belief that they can win domestic arguments by logic!

What is to be done? Let me suggest two guidelines.

First, make understanding a priority. In a conflict, it is easy to want, above all, to demonstrate that your own point of view is wise, good and right. But it is far better to forget making self-justification your goal – remember, in a marriage, winning is not the issue – and instead try to quietly ask directed questions to find out the real issues. These might be along the lines of 'What is the problem?'

'Is that the real problem?' and 'What answer would you like?'

Second, determine those areas where you agree. You will, hopefully, never disagree with your spouse 100 per cent, so try to find out those areas where there is agreement. Such a strategy has several advantages. First, it is positive in that it highlights those features that unite you, rather than those that divide you. Secondly, it helps identify the specific problem and points out the area where hard work is needed.

A genuinely useful conflict resolution technique is to try to express the problem in your own words. So, when your spouse says something like, 'I hate this house – it feels like a weight tied around my neck,' you might respond with something such as, 'Okay, so what I understand you to be saying is that you find that the upkeep and maintenance of this house is physically draining you. Is that right?' This kind of response does several things. It shows that you have heard what is being said. Trying to express the problem another way forces you to identify with the issues and, very importantly, to see things through your spouse's eyes. Because it is a neutral request for information, rather than a judgemental statement such as 'Tough, it was your decision to buy it!' it builds bonds, rather than breaks them.

Furthermore, the perspective you come up with may help your spouse to see the problem from a different point of view.

3. Aim for a resolution that cures, not simply calms

Because a marital conflict hurts so much, it is tempting to adopt any strategy that promises to ease matters. The danger here is that you settle for a temporary solution rather than a permanent resolution. This is similar to

someone who, after injuring themselves, decides to treat
the pain with aspirin instead of going to the doctor. It is
quicker, easier, and may
deal with the symptoms,
but if there is a real problem
then it is no solution, and
may in the long run make
matters worse. Conflict
suppression may appear to
be the same as conflict
resolution, but it is not. This
sort of temporary and
superficial treatment can easily produce a situation where
the problem resurfaces again.

*As Athenodorus was
taking his leave of Caesar,
'Remember,' said he,
'Caesar, whenever you are
angry, to say or do nothing
before you have repeated
the four-and-twenty letters
to yourself.'*
Plutarch (46–120)

Do remember, too, that you may have to resolve two
separate things: the real issue of the conflict and the
emotions that have arisen from it. Husbands often fall
short in this area, because they tend to see the issues
while overlooking the associated emotional hurts. The
result is that while they may successfully resolve the
issues, they may fail to address the emotional wounds.

4. Keep it cool

On the surface, to suggest that you keep cool when you
argue may seem to be foolish advice. After all, isn't a
conflict about feeling angry? Yet conflicts can occur
without anger and are always resolved much more easily
in its absence. Anger is rarely a productive emotion. It
increases the temperature of any conflict, makes forgiveness harder and makes it far more likely that unwise or
hurtful things will be said. To have a conflict when you
are angry is to lift the restrictions off your emotions and
to fight with the gloves off.

It is important that, as far as possible, you remain

emotionally controlled in an argument. That may mean both controlling your own anger and avoiding saying anything that will make your spouse angry. There are various ways and means of doing this. For instance, conflict resolution studies point out that there are ways of addressing issues that can help reduce anger. So, for instance, to say things like 'you should' or 'you shouldn't' tend to get people annoyed, because that is the way in which, as children, they were addressed by their parents. 'You always' or 'you never' are also phrases to be avoided, as they always indicate an attempt to broaden the conflict out and to turn challenge or complaint into criticism. In contrast, making 'I feel' statements to express your feelings or your response helps neutralise anger.

Because anger is so dangerous and so counter-productive to solving arguments, if you or your spouse have become very angry with each other then you may see that you have reached a state where *Never yell at each other unless the home is on fire.* resolving the conflict is, for the moment, impossible. The best thing may be to take time out and let tempers cool.

Part of keeping it cool is not just doing what you can to prevent escalation – it is, at the same time, trying to find a way out of the conflict. Some couples evolve mechanisms of defusing the anger in an argument. So, in one marriage, when he wants to get out of the argument he may shrug his shoulders, sigh and say, 'Oh, what the heck! I'm not arguing. Do it your way.' Or, she may just pull a face and stick her tongue out, with the result that they end up laughing together. For each, these are their own very different ways of saying that they have higher priorities than continuing an argument. I suspect that, given time, most couples evolve their own defusing mechanisms: perhaps holding hands or stroking a shoulder. But you may have to work at creating and recognising them.

5. Be fair and honest

It is vital that, in marriage, conflicts are conducted with fairness. It is a universal human temptation to use any tactic and any weapon in order to win an argument. But in all conflicts, and especially those in marriage, there must be rules and those rules must be kept.

It is impossible to list all the unfair and dishonest tactics that can be employed in disputes but let me list some general rules.

- Apply excuses equally. Do not say, 'Well, I've been stressed at work' without recognising that your spouse may have been as well.
- Never exaggerate or lie. It is easy to try to bolster your case by saying things like 'Of course, I told you I wanted to go out tonight' when, in reality, you merely hinted at this.
- Never put the worst possible interpretation on what your spouse says. So, if one partner says, 'I feel that you don't give me a chance to be involved in decisions' it is hardly fair for the other to say, 'Oh, so you think that I bully you?'

If we are unfair, it is almost certain that our spouse will notice it and feel angered. To fight unfairly is one of the surest ways of increasing the temperature of an argument.

6. Don't expand the conflict

It's a good rule to stay focused on the issue at hand and to resist the temptation to broaden a conflict. If the issue is last month's overspending, then it shouldn't be expanded to bring in her reckless purchases during last year's sales or his failure to get a better paid job.

Stay on target and don't open a second front. If other issues emerge, then promise to look at them another time. It is all too easy for a small argument in one specific area of a marriage to broaden out into a global warfare that runs wild across almost every area of married life. Stay focused on the essential problem.

7. *Avoid allegations, insults and ridicule*

Related to the previous points is the necessity of ensuring that you don't resort to attacking your spouse. This is especially difficult in a culture that says that it is better to express your feelings than to keep them bottled up inside. The reality is that it is far better

> *I love being married. It's so great to find the one special person you want to annoy for the rest of your life.*
>
> **Rita Rudner**

to hold your tongue and think how to most sensitively and tactfully convey your opinion later. If you must criticise, do it lovingly and preferably not during an argument. In the heat of battle, even a well-meant and constructive criticism can easily be misidentified as a hurtful insult.

Insults or allegations made in the heat of an argument may sting and fester for the rest of a marriage. To say to someone 'you're a failure' or 'you only married me for my money' or 'you're frigid' are words whose wounds, even if they heal, will leave long-lasting scars. We always need to remember that what is said in haste is often repented of at leisure and that once spoken, a word cannot be recalled. Remember that in marriage, you are far better off losing an argument than winning it with insults.

Ridicule is also a weapon that ought to be banned by the marital equivalent of the Geneva Convention. It may be amusing as part of a television comedy script, but in real life it is rarely of benefit and frequently causes lasting harm. Anyway, it also backfires – if your spouse is that bad then why were you so stupid as to marry them?

8. *Be prompt in seeking and giving forgiveness*

Built into all of us is a tremendous reluctance to admit that we have done wrong and that we need to ask for forgiveness. In marriage, such reluctance can be catastrophic. When you have done something wrong, admit it, apologise and ask for forgiveness. Don't defend the indefensible! In fact, to actually apologise regularly in a marriage is a sign of strength, not weakness; it indicates a degree of security. And if it is a good idea to be quick to admit your own guilt and ask for forgiveness, it is also a good policy to be similarly quick to forgive. Part of the process of being prepared to give forgiveness is to be prepared to admit personal blame. Not all wrongs in a marriage are the responsibility of one party alone and sometimes, blame must be shared.

9. *Try to impose limits on any conflict*

If conflicts are allowed to continue then they may last for a long time, and the longer they last, the more chance there is that they will become worse, rather than better. While there should be time for reflection and discussion, it is a good idea, as I suggested earlier, to set limits to conflicts. Some couples, for instance, may set a time limit of 10 p.m. and refuse to ever argue beyond that point. For a Christian couple who always end a day with prayer together (a good idea anyway), that activity marks a natural end for conflict. The advice of the Apostle Paul was to fix a time limit to quarrels, 'And don't sin by letting anger gain control over you. Don't let the sun go down while you are still angry, for anger gives a mighty foothold to the Devil' (Eph. 4:26,27). Others refuse to allow arguments into the bedroom, so that when one party goes to bed the matter is closed.

Another rule is to never part from each other with a conflict unresolved. There are at least two good arguments for this rule. The first is that unresolved arguments in marriage are a major factor in making extramarital affairs attractive. The second, which some may find morbid, is that if there was a conflict that was left unresolved, and then one partner died, it would be a double tragedy. To be bereaved must be hard enough, but to know that when you parted for the last time you were still arguing, is something that would make it even worse. Forgive before you part.

10. End it properly

I have already given as a principle the need to make resolution a goal and I don't need to restate that. But let me make three further suggestions. One: when a conflict has ended, ensure that it stays ended. Never revive an issue that you have resolved. Don't dig up dead bodies. Two: review what happened. You certainly ought to do that on your own, but if it can be done without a renewed flare-up of the conflict, do it with your spouse as well. Ask yourself whether the conflict could have been avoided, whether you could have resolved it another way, and what lessons there are for any future conflicts. The old and wise rule is that if you don't learn from your mistakes, then you end up repeating them. Three: make a special effort to regain lost ground in your marriage. If you think of your marriage as being like a bank account, a conflict is like a sudden, massive withdrawal, and unless your account is boosted, you may soon drift into further trouble. So, do something that you both enjoy and make a real effort at your marriage. Get it back on track.

Finally, what if, despite the best of intentions and a lot of discussion, you still don't agree? I suggest that you review the issues and try to identify exactly where you agree and disagree. Where is it that you are stuck? For the moment, agree to differ and take a break of hours or even days and then come back to the issues and try to resolve them again. If all else fails, you may need to bring in someone else, even a marriage counsellor, to help resolve matters.

Handling marriage conflict: some Christian distinctives

Although I have made some reference to Christian attitudes and practices, I think that what I have said applies to all marriages, whether they are Christian or not. However, in a number of ways, Christians should be able to go further when it comes to handling disputes.

Ask for God's help through prayer. God is concerned, and it is good to pray to him about the issues. Mind you, having the right attitude in prayer is important: it is all too easy for us to pray to God as if we are trying to persuade him to be on our side. To do this is to abuse the privilege of prayer and to totally fail to recognise who God is. It is far better to come humbly to God, confessing our failings, asking for his help to heal matters, and being prepared for him to show us where we are wrong. There ought also to be a realisation that to pray about a marriage conflict should not be a substitute for working to solve it. There is sometimes the danger that prayer can be resorted to as an act of laziness, almost as if we are saying, 'Sorting out all this is too much like hard work for me – you do it, God.' Here, as elsewhere in life, work and prayer go together.

Remember that, as a Christian, you are under a particular obligation to forgive. As God has forgiven you generously, so you must also forgive generously. In the Lord's Prayer (Mt. 6:12 and also 6:14,15) Jesus links, in rather a challenging fashion, our own forgiveness with our forgiveness of others. Linked to forgiveness should be the realisation that it is God's job to judge, not ours.

Seek God's power through his Holy Spirit to deal with the issues that arise out of the conflict. It is easy to say in despair, 'It's no good, I can't change' or 'It's hopeless'. Humanly speaking that may be so, but the great thing about being a Christian is that 'humanly speaking' is not the end of the story.

A Special Issue: Help! I Married the Wrong Person

I think it is right to consider here one particular nagging doubt that can strike someone in a marriage and which can have devastating results. It is the concern that they made a terrible mistake in their choice of spouse and that they are married to the wrong person. I have put the subject here because I suspect that it is often during conflicts that such feelings of having committed a terrible blunder first arise.

For someone to feel that they have married the wrong person must be terrible. Let me cautiously offer some suggestions in this area.

- There is an element of modern mythology here that needs to be confronted. The current view is that marriage is a lottery in which success depends largely on finding just the right partner. Get the right ticket and you are fine – get the wrong one and you've had it. Yet the reality is that it is not so much a business of finding the right person to marry, but one of being the right person in marriage.

- You need to be aware that to say, 'I've made a mistake, I married the wrong person!' can be a self-fulfilling prophecy. Once you believe it, then it is all too easy to give up. It is like saying to yourself at work, 'I am in the wrong job and I'm going to fail at it': keep repeating it for long enough and you will almost certainly find yourself faced with failure. Frankly, the thought that you married the wrong person is one that is so unhelpful that I would suggest that you evict it from your mind as soon as it appears. In fact, I would try to prevent it ever taking root by acquiring the practice of praising your spouse and being grateful for them.

- Sadly, I also have to say that the idea that 'I married the wrong person' can be a useful excuse for marriage failure. Instead of someone having to admit that they are failing to make their marriage work, it is all too easy for them to say instead, 'I made an error of judgement in the past'. Applied with a bit of careful spin – 'I was badly advised,' 'we were young', 'I was too hasty' – even someone who has been responsible for the wreckage of a marriage can appear to be merely an innocent victim of bad luck and misjudgement.

- Because of today's total confusion about what love is, many people expect their married life to continue forever on the cloud of happy emotions with which, presumably, it started. When that romantic euphoria ends, they can easily conclude that the reason their emotions have changed is that they made a mistake.

'Surely,' they say sadly, 'if I had married the right person, I would still feel in love.' Yet, as I have pointed out, feelings change and evolve. The core of a marriage must be built on commitment, not feelings.

- Remember that to divorce and have another go at marriage is no guarantee of success. Part of our society's view about marriage is that you may need to try, and try again, until you succeed. The reality is that second marriages often fail as well. A new start with someone else may look attractive when you are in a conflict situation, but the reality is that history may very well repeat itself. It is all too frequent for problems that exist in one marriage to be transferred to the next one.

- Remember that the basis of your marriage is the sworn agreement you made to love each other. Hold firm to that and press on in your marriage. You may well find that, if you and your spouse are really determined to make it work, that it will indeed work.

Finally, remember that there may be the possibility of a new start within marriage. You may need to seek the help of a counsellor, to ask for forgiveness and to work with renewed effort at loving your spouse, but I believe that making a new start is possible. If you are a Christian then you have grounds for special encouragement – you have access to God's wisdom, power and love. And remember that Jesus has a proven record in healing the sick and raising the dead.

Chapter 5

How to Affair-Proof Your Marriage (1)
The Causes of Affairs

As she put away her car keys, Liz paused and looked around appreciatively at the house and the garden. Everything was bathed in the warm golden sunlight of the summer's afternoon, the lawns were freshly mown, and she was aware of the smell of honeysuckle, the hum of insects and the coo of doves in the trees. After the noise, fume and chaos of London, she rejoiced to be back to her quiet, scented and well-ordered haven. She decided that there would be time for her and Dave to sit outside and have coffee together after supper; the church meeting was not until eight. She began to walk to the door.

As Liz walked into the house, she was struck by the strange emptiness. The mail on the mat was untouched.

'Dave?' she called out, 'Dave?' but there was no answer.

'Strange,' she said to herself, wishing she had checked the garage to see if his car was there. In the hallway, she noticed that there was no message on the answerphone. Puzzled, and struggling with a sense of unease, she went upstairs to the bedroom.

Something was wrong.

The suitcases were missing from above the wardrobe. The

cupboards where Dave kept his clothes were wide open and the shelves were oddly bare. 'Burglars?' She thought in alarm, until she turned to see a necklace and bracelet lying untouched on her dressing table.

Trying to defy an overpowering sense of doom, Liz ran down to the kitchen. There was an envelope on the table addressed to her in Dave's handwriting. She ripped it open, her fingers scrabbling, and as she pulled out the single sheet of paper, she was aware of something rolling out on to the table with a soft metallic clunk.

She ignored it, reading the letter, desperately fighting off panic and tears, barely able to take in the words and what they meant.

Dave wrote that he had 'been having an affair with a work colleague'; he 'had to choose between Liz and her' and he had decided that it was time 'to move on'.

Liz, blinking away tears, was aware of her pounding heart.

It was 'unfortunate' Dave said; he wished 'that it could have been otherwise'. His solicitor would be in touch, but she would be provided for.

'Thanks for the good times,' he ended, 'I hope it works out for you. Sorry, Dave'.

As the letter dropped out of her shaking hands, Liz saw, on the table, the golden band of his wedding ring.

Introduction

It is, I suppose, just possible that someone reading this book thinks they can skip this chapter and the next. Perhaps they are in the first happy flush of marriage or so firmly convinced of their love's strength that they feel that what happened to Dave and Liz could only happen to other people. If this is you, let me simply and bluntly say: 'Get real!'

Actually, I would go further: by adopting such an attitude you might easily be laying yourself wide open to potential disaster. 'I just can't believe that it could have happened to us' is one of those tearful expressions that is heard all too often by those in marriage counselling.

We have to concede that today, in modern Western society, affairs represent a real threat to any marriage. It is not entirely the fault of our society: I believe that given the way that human nature is, the inclination to have an affair is built into all of us. Marriages have always been prone to affairs, it is just that they have never been easier to have than they are now. Indeed, one of the major shifts in society has been the acceptance, and even expectation, of affairs. Forty years ago, all the pressures of society were towards the stability of marriage, and to have an affair or to get a divorce was, in a very real sense, to go against the flow. The change in the last few decades has been remarkable. Now there are no such stabilising forces: indeed the cultural pressures today are such as to encourage splitting up, having an affair or letting a marriage fail. Nowadays, to change your partner is seen as just something that you do in the course of a lifetime. It is part of reinventing yourself and, from the way some people talk, it is only slightly more traumatic than throwing out your wardrobe and starting all over again. Today, to work at staying married is to go against the flow.

What I want to do in this chapter is to look at why affairs happen, ask whether they are inevitable, look at some of the attitudes that cause affairs and then suggest how we can prevent them. I want to leave the delicate subject of handling an affair until the next chapter. But first, I want to look at what we mean by 'an affair'.

What is an Affair?

What constitutes an affair? This is one of those questions that seems obvious – after all, we all know what an affair is. But do we? Think about the following situations:

- Bill is a married man who, on an overseas business trip, has a drunken one-night stand with a prostitute. He never even finds out her name and next morning is appalled by his hazy memories of what happened. Years later, it remains his only sexual venture outside marriage.

- Angie has been married for 20 years. For half of that time, Jeff, her male colleague has been her closest confidante, encourager and supporter. He now provides the psychological and emotional intimacy that her husband used to. There is no sexual relationship between her and Jeff.

Clearly, Bill has had an affair, but has Angie?

In trying to answer this, I think it may be helpful to do some hard thinking. My definition of marriage is: 'Marriage is a legally recognised, lifelong union between one man and one woman involving psychological, sexual, social and spiritual bonds.' These four dimensions of a marriage, like embankments or walls, also define the bounds or limits of marriage. With that image in mind, let me suggest that we can identify two different sorts of affair.

The adulterous affair is where a sexual liaison has taken place. This is probably what most people think of when they think of an affair. Incidentally, it is probably foolish to be too specific about what precise form of sexual activity has to occur to make it adultery. As a good non-legal rule, if you require privacy for you to do it, then it's adultery. Adultery is serious – make no mistake. Even

if it is only a one-night stand and there are no complica-
tions to do with pregnancy or a sexually transmitted
disease, an act of adultery thrusts a knife into the heart of
any marriage. The sexual union is so central to the
intimacy of a marriage that no third party can be allowed
to intrude into it.

The non-adulterous affair is where, although there is
no sexual act, the psychological, social or even spiritual
boundaries of a marriage are broken by one party's
relationship with another person. Although perhaps less
drastic than actual adultery – it rarely makes it into the
divorce courts or the newspapers – such non-adulterous
affairs are still unwelcome and damaging intrusions into
marriage. Defining exactly whether this sort of affair has
taken place is far from easy and it probably varies from
marriage to marriage. The key issue would be whether
the spouse affected finds it objectionable.

Both an adulterous and a non-adulterous affair
damage a marriage in different ways. It is not even easy
to say which is the most damaging. Although Bill's one-
off fling was adultery, it might actually have been less
harmful to his marriage than Angie's ten-year-long non-
adulterous relationship with a colleague was to hers. But
to try to determine which sort of affair is more harmful is
about as sensible as deciding whether a bout of
depression is worse than breaking your legs. Both
adulterous and non-adulterous affairs involve the basic
and down-to-earth definition of an affair; they are
cheating on your partner. In a marriage, your spouse
comes first. Whenever they come second you have got
the order very wrong.

While we are thinking about the 'types of affairs', it is
worth saying that there are two extreme forms of
adultery. One is the sudden, impulsive, hot-blooded
sexual encounter: the single act of lust in a moment of

folly. The other is the coldly planned and pursued affair that, generally under the cover of lies, goes on for weeks or months. Now both are wrong and I defend neither, but I think most people would consider the second type worse. To add deliberate deceit to adultery is to make things far worse.

I need to say here that while affairs in the past were overwhelmingly between people of the opposing sex, this is no longer the case. You increasingly hear of marriage break-ups where the husband has run off with a man or the wife with another woman. Actually, I'm not convinced that these are, in themselves, fundamentally different from the 'traditional' affair, but they do seem to generate even more hurt and pain. I believe that what I have written below applies to any sort of affair.

Are Affairs Inevitable?

The two views that I consider unhealthy and potentially very dangerous to marriage are those of the Cold Cynic and the Rosy Romantic. The Cold Cynics accept that affairs are, like sore throats or toothache – a fact of life – they turn up sooner or later. Of course, to adopt such an outlook is to accept that affairs will happen. All you can do is to prepare for the worst and try to minimise the damage when it occurs.

The Rosy Romantics adopt the opposite attitude and refuse to consider even the possibility of an affair. Affairs, they say defiantly, happen in other people's marriages, they do not happen to us – *we* are different – *we* are immune. Actually, the current climate is so corro-

> *But the man who commits adultery is an utter fool, for he destroys his own soul. Wounds and constant disgrace are his lot.*
>
> **Proverbs 6:32,33**

sive towards marriage that few Rosy Romantics say this sort of thing publicly. But there must be people who still believe it, because marriage counsellors frequently counsel couples who shake their heads in disbelief and say things like, 'I could never have imagined that it was going to happen to us. We were going to be different.'

Incidentally, there is a peculiarly dangerous religious version of being a Rosy Romantic. This is to say that yes, we know that love isn't enough but we have God as well and he will keep our marriage intact. Well, he may indeed do so, but I don't think it's wise to presume. I believe God can keep my car from being stolen when I park it, but I still lock it. Faith and naivety are actually two separate things. With the pressures within our culture now, affairs can – and do – happen among religious couples.

There is an alternative to both Rosy Romanticism and Cold Cynicism which I call, by way of shorthand, Holy Realism. Holy Realism holds together both pessimism and optimism. It recognises with the Rosy Romantics the great value of marriage, but it agrees with the Cold Cynics that there are pressures on marriage and that affairs are a real threat. But Holy Realism says that, through God's grace and power and with hard work, these tendencies to marital destruction can be overcome.

Holy Realism occurs within the Bible. The teaching of the Bible is that every human being is flawed by a tendency to rebel against what is right and that this tendency runs throughout all that we think and do. In its teaching that even our thoughts are contaminated, the Bible pre-empts much of Freud's thinking. The classic example is that of David, the devout king of Israel who lived around 1000 BC. In 2 Samuel chapter 11, the Bible recounts, with blunt honesty, how David, in spite of being a genuine believer in God, committed adultery and then, in order to cover it up, lied and eventually arranged a murder. The Bible goes on to tell how, after being rebuked by God, David repented and was forgiven by God. Nevertheless, the bitter consequences of his actions echoed on for generations. There are many lessons in this story, but one stands out above all: if adultery can happen to David, it can happen to anybody.

Are affairs inevitable? No, but neither are they impossible. None of us has a marriage that has a guaranteed immunity to affairs. Affair-proofing is not a strategy needed only by those with weak marriages; it is needed by everybody who is married.

Looking for Trouble: Six Conditions that can Lead to Affairs

Affairs do not 'just happen'. Look into an affair and you will find that there were causes and origins; the trouble had been quietly brewing for some time.

In this section, I want to look at these causes and consider six conditions that, if not addressed, can create an environment in which affairs can easily occur. These are lust, loneliness, boredom, insecurity, laziness and escapism. Let me deal with them in turn.

1. Lust

A passing alien casting tentacled eyes over the magazines available today on the shelves of any of our

A lot of people have sex on the brain and that's the worst place to have it.

newsagents, might easily conclude that the human race believed sex was the supreme purpose of life. Whether on billboards, magazine covers, television or T-shirts –

encouragement to work up a sexual hunger is everywhere.

It is not surprising then, that most people would probably consider lust as the major cause of adultery. I wouldn't want to disagree: it is certainly one of the main reasons why men have affairs. Yet, contrary to what some fiction – mostly written by men for men – says, I do not believe that lust is the major explanation for why women have affairs. But lust is a serious problem and any extramarital relationship with lust as a cause is likely to have adulterous results.

Before I argue against lust, I should point out that, along with most Christian writers down the ages, I do not include sexual desire within marriage as lust. I believe that such desires are God-given, good and to be appreciated. To lust is to desire sexually what is not yours to have.

Now modern Western society generally puts forward the view that ideas don't matter and that therefore lust is no big deal. What you can't see, it is argued, won't hurt you. But, as so often, we are inconsistent because, deep down, there is an unease about lust. Few people will admit to it themselves, and while a woman might appreciate being told that a man 'fancied her', to be told that he 'lusted for her' might have her checking that her door is locked. In an age of widespread sexual crime, there is a suspicion about lust even amongst those who consider themselves to be liberally-minded. I think these misgivings are well founded. Lust is both harmful and dangerous. Let me give my reasons for saying so:

Judge: So why are you seeking a divorce?
Woman: Because all my husband wants to do is make love.
Judge: Most women would be pleased about that.
Woman: They are. That's why I want a divorce!

- Lust totally distorts relationships between men and women. When lust is let loose, values such as companionship, respect and emotional intimacy go out of the window to be replaced by a single, basic, hormone-driven desire. People become simply the containers for sexual pleasure.

- Lust distorts who we are. The criteria on which we assess who we are becomes reduced to whether or not we are people that others can lust after. Our self-esteem therefore becomes based almost entirely on looks and not on personality. Every person is assessed only on his, or her, sexual attractiveness.

- Lust even distorts the very thing that it focuses on, sex. The sexual act is just one part of a loving union of emotional and psychological intimacies between two people. Lust selfishly rips sex out of that context. I suspect – but cannot prove – that those whose lives are dominated by lust do not (except perhaps in a very basic physical sense) make the best lovers. They are too selfish for a start.

- Lust fuels dissatisfaction within marriage. After all, no one's real-life spouse can be expected to compete with those flawlessly athletic, eternally youthful and sexually insatiable creatures of our imaginations.

- Lust is destructive to the one who lusts. By engaging in lust, you are working up an appetite that can never, except very briefly, be satisfied. Lust is as satisfying as drinking salt water. It is addictive and enslaving.

- Thoughts do lead to actions. For example, trial reports of people convicted of sexual crimes commonly reveal a history of the use of pornography. It is hard to demonstrate that their use of pornography is the cause of their criminal behaviour, but it does suggest that pornography may not be a harmless recreational activity.

- Those who take Jesus' teaching seriously should note his strong statements about the need to guard the mind. He specifically made the point in the case of adultery. Listen to what he said: 'You have heard that the law of Moses says, "Do not commit adultery." But I say, anyone who even looks at a woman with lust in his eye has already committed adultery with her in his heart.' (Mt. 5:27,28). The desire, he is saying, is the seed of the action; there is not a vast difference between the real adulterer and one who enjoys mental adultery but doesn't have the opportunity or the courage to carry it out.

Having said that, let me expose a few fallacies about lust:

Fallacy 1: A husband lusts simply because the quantity or quality of sex in the marriage bed is inadequate. False. Like many appetites, the more you have, the more you want. Yes, a great sex life helps bond a marriage in many ways, but lust and affairs can still occur where there is good marital sex. In fact, lust is, in some way, independent of the physical need: there are many sad and pathetic figures around who, long after any physical capacity for sex has gone, are still driven by their lust.

Lust: an undress rehearsal for adultery.

Fallacy 2: I can't do anything about lust – it's the way I am. Let me say here that, as far as I am aware, erotic thoughts go through the minds of most men and women a lot of the time. But lust is something more than that: lust is seizing hold of the erotic thought, dwelling on it and even working it up. The wisest action is to deal firmly with lust and, whenever it arises, quickly show it the door. And before you give up in despair, let me tell you that one of the biggest of many fallacies around today is the one that says that you can't change. You can – God says so.

Fallacy 3: Lust is good for my marriage. I suppose the idea here is that lust is a sort of mental warm-up exercise for the marriage bed. Well, if you consider the sexual act as being just

> *But remember that the temptations that come into your life are no different from what others experience. And God is faithful. He will keep the temptation from becoming so strong that you can't stand up against it. When you are tempted, he will show you a way out so that you will not give in to it.*
>
> **1 Corinthians 10:13**

a matter of gymnastics, then you may have a point. But if you take the view that I do, that it is a part of an emotional and physical union, then what lust may (and only may) give in terms of physical performance, it takes away elsewhere. Of course, in any long-term marriage there will be times where the sexual arousal of one's spouse may not occur automatically and may have to be encouraged. But there are right and wrong ways of working up sexual arousal within marriage and to do it through encouraging lust (remember: the sexual desire for what is not yours to have) is to venture into dangerous territory. It is a bit like using petrol to light a fire – it works, but the side effects can be unwelcome.

Lust is so much a part of our culture that many of us have probably never given it serious thought. Yet, if you want a satisfying and long-lasting marriage then I would urge you, at the very least, to think carefully about it. I would go further: if you have acquired the habit of lusting, try to get out of it. Don't feed it by pornography or dwelling on sexual thoughts in your mind. And if you haven't acquired the habit of lust, make every effort not to get it.

2. *Loneliness*

Compared to lust, loneliness may seem an unspectacular factor in affairs. But the drive to overcome loneliness is a powerful one and can easily lead to affairs. I suspect that in women it is loneliness, rather than lust, which is the main reason for affairs. Loneliness is the feeling that you don't really matter to anyone, of not being significant, of being isolated – of being alone. There are two types of loneliness: *physical* and *psychological*.

Physical loneliness is probably the kind of loneliness that most of us would immediately think of. Here, for one reason or another, there is an inadequate level of physical contact within the marriage. An obvious example would be where a husband or wife is away on an extended business trip and both of them may feel lonely. A subtler – but no less dangerous situation – could occur where a husband or wife commutes to work and spends long hours away from home. They rise early and return late in the evening, too tired to do anything except slump in a chair with the TV remote control. They are absent partners in their marriage.

No less dangerous is *psychological loneliness*. Here, there may be a physical presence, but there is an emotional gap. It is summed up in those clichés that are so common in television and film dramas about affairs: 'I can talk to you about things that I can't talk to him about'; 'I know she isn't really interested in how I feel' and 'He doesn't understand me'. It is a powerful pressure for an affair. For instance, take a woman who is very musical: for her, music is something that lies at the deepest part of her personality. Now imagine that she is married to a man who does not care for music and has no understanding of what it means to her. And now imagine further that, in the course of a tour with her choir, she meets a man who is on her wavelength and who loves music in the same way. Can you sense the appeal of a deep psychological and emotional intimacy?

Loneliness is a fertile soil for an affair – whether adulterous or non-adulterous – to blossom in. If you are in a marriage, you need to think carefully about whether you are allowing either sort of loneliness to creep in. Communication – verbal, emotional and physical – is the best antidote to loneliness, so keep the links to your spouse strong. If you don't have common interests, try to acquire some.

I don't want to underestimate the problem of loneliness: it is a serious one and anyone who suffers from it has my sympathies. Yet, I have to say that an affair is not the answer. To treat loneliness by having an affair is as sensible as burning your house down to keep warm. You need to make friends, not have an affair.

3. Boredom

A third factor is, quite simply, boredom. It lies behind the well-known expression 'the seven-year itch'. Mind you, these days I suspect that this has been reduced to about three years and six months. This boredom may be part of the marriage itself: perhaps the novelty of being married has worn off and the initial infatuation has faded away. This boredom may, however, be less to do with the marriage and more to do with work or life in general. At work, every day brings the same mindless, repetitive tasks and there is nothing to look forward to except the slow ticking away of the seasons. An affair promises an escape from such a purposeless existence. It offers excitement and change and it can be

Society is now one polished horde, Formed of two mighty tribes, the Bores and the Bored.

Byron, *Don Juan*

seen as an adventure, a novelty and a challenge. Bored with the office? Have an affair! But like many other stimulants, there is a heavy price to pay.

With boredom, as with loneliness, we have a problem to which an affair pretends to be a solution. It isn't, of course: the solution to boredom lies elsewhere. And of course, if you get into the habit of having an affair every time you are bored then your new relationship may not last long. Once the novelty fades, the boredom may be back. Boredom is one of the forces that drives the serial adulterer: the sad man or woman who goes from affair to affair.

If boredom does strike your life, let me urge you to seek out and treat the reasons for it. Perhaps you should find a job that offers new challenges or a change of scene. Alternatively, why not take up a new activity in your spare time? Having an affair is a poor remedy for boredom.

4. Insecurity

Sometimes people are tempted to have an affair or to flirt just to try to prove something. It is an attempt to make themselves feel secure. This is often associated with the celebrated mid-life crisis. In a culture that has elevated 'sexiness' above almost everything, the damaging effects of middle age can be unnerving. What greater reassurance can there be that we are still sexually attractive than to have an affair: preferably, of course, with someone who is younger? And, of course, if there is any degree of infatuation, then an affair may indeed give the illusion of

> *It is the fear of middle age in the young, of old age in the middle-aged, which is the prime cause of infidelity, that infallible rejuvenator.*
>
> **Cyril Connolly**

rolling back the years. One day you are in late middle age, grinding your way forward to retirement in a nine-to-five job, the next – courtesy of your little fling – you are back in your twenties again, with your hormones flowing and your glands pumping.

Yet, of course, it is all an illusion: affairs do not reverse time and ageing continues unabated. In fact, in yet another of the ironies attached to marriage, the stresses and strains of an affair are likely to increase – not decrease – the effects of age.

Incidentally, people suffering from this condition are actually the worst sort of people to have affairs with. They only want to prove a point, and once that is proved, what is there to keep them involved? For them, having an affair is like climbing Mount Everest – they want to be able to say they did it but they have not the slightest intention of staying any longer than it takes to place the flag!

Let me point out that, again, we have a situation where an affair presents itself as an answer to a problem. It isn't of course – we all have to come to terms with insecurity, ageing and mortality, but an affair is not an answer – it is, at best, a distraction of the worst kind.

5. Laziness

Laziness may seem a strange condition to mention, yet I think it is an important factor in explaining why some affairs occur. You see it is often the case that a husband or wife finds that their marriage is not the lifelong bed of roses they expected and that it requires more hard work than they are prepared to give it. And if, at this time, the opportunity of another relationship appears, then it may seem to them to offer a far easier option than working at their marriage.

For centuries, people have dreamed of how to make a perpetual motion machine. Such a device – which remains pure fantasy – would run forever without anybody ever having to put any energy or work into it. A 'perpetual motion machine fantasy' widely occurs within marriages, so that couples imagine that no effort is needed to keep things going. Now, this is utter foolishness. To want a marriage to work implies that you are prepared to work at the marriage. Successful marriages do not occur automatically, they take effort. Show me a successful marriage and I will show you one where there has been a great deal of hard work!

Laziness presents a danger, because an affair promises an effortless alternative to labouring on in a marriage. When your marriage can seem like a weary hike up a steep slope, then an affair can look like a smooth path that runs gently downhill: a labour-free option. But of course, as with the other conditions, there is a deceptive fallacy here. Even if, for argument's sake, you were to get into this apparently zero-effort affair, I can guarantee you that, sooner or later, it would require hard work and this path too would start to wind uphill steeply. And then what do you do? Look for yet another softer option and start all over again?

Laziness is probably the other major reason why some people go from affair to affair. They are never prepared to make the effort for a relationship to mature and develop. When the going gets tough, they press the 'eject' button and bail out. Rather than being people to be envied, those men and women who go through strings of affairs are to be pitied. They suffer from an inability to stick at any relationship long enough to take it on beyond the initial stage.

6. Escapism

A final condition, escapism, is a cousin of laziness. It is to seek, consciously or subconsciously, an escape route from a situation where a difficult action is required. Let me give you an illustration from outside marriage. Imagine that at work, you have a complicated and painful letter to write. It needs to be done, but you know it will trigger a confrontation that you would prefer not to face. Suddenly you will find that all sorts of other projects seem to be more pressing: the computer needs backing up, the accounts must be done, the furniture rearranged. Of course, these other projects are a distraction, and what you are really doing is trying to escape from your responsibility. By ignoring the problem, you hope that it will go away or someone else will do it.

This sort of thing is all too common in marriage. Perhaps there is a hard decision within the relationship that needs making, but the party concerned prefers not to face it. Or maybe a conflict needs to be dealt with which is just too hard to face. Something else – anything else – is preferable. An affair seems to provide the perfect escape route. It offers a diversion and a postponement of the hard decision.

> *There are a lot of marriages today that break up just at the point where they could mature and deepen. We are taught to quit when it hurts. But often it is the times of pain that produce the most growth in a relationship.*
>
> **Madeleine L'Engle**

As with laziness, this is a condition that has to be fought. Beware the temptation to dodge hard issues. Face up to the things you have to do and tackle them head on. To dodge every challenge and difficulty is no way to run a life and is certainly no way to mature.

Taking preventive action against dangerous conditions

Lust, loneliness, boredom, insecurity, laziness and escapism are conditions that we need to watch out for if we are to affair-proof marriages. I suspect that most – if not all – of these conditions occur to some extent in all marriages at some time or another. Yet, the danger lies in the fact that they are generally not taken seriously. We may decide that they are no big deal; that we can handle them.

> *Watch your thoughts, they become words.*
> *Watch your words, they become actions.*
> *Watch your actions, they become habits.*
> *Watch your habits, they become character.*
> *Watch your character, they become your destiny.*

My boredom, my desire to prove myself, my hankerings to opt out of issues in my marriage are, we say, a minor thing. They are just daydreaming or having fantasies – a perfectly harmless vice.

But are such thoughts so harmless? Here we come to another important truth that our society has lost: we need to guard our minds. Over the years, whenever a society has talked about morals, it has always talked about actions. After all, it's hard to police or penalise thoughts. So most people would say that you could think what you like – just don't do it. But thoughts are the parents of actions: no one is surprised when it turns out that a murderer had been thinking murderous thoughts about their victim for years. Jesus taught that the heart was the root of action, and also deserved to be judged. 'But evil words come from an evil heart and defile the person who says them. For from the heart come evil thoughts, murder, adultery, all other sexual immorality, theft, lying, and slander.' (Mt. 15:18,19). And, as we have just seen, Jesus specifically made the point in the case of adultery.

The desire, he said, is the parent of the action. There is not a vast difference between the one who enjoys mental adultery, but doesn't have the opportunity or the courage to carry it out, and someone who expresses that desire in action.

A thought may take a person prisoner.

In other words, the secret to preventing affairs caused by lust, loneliness or boredom and so on is to deal with thoughts immediately. 'Don't even think about it!' we might warn someone. But it is not a bad idea for us to direct such words to ourselves. A Christian would go further still and seek the strength of God's Holy Spirit to help them deal with the matter. Another suggestion, and one that I will discuss later, is that it is actually no bad thing to let our thought life be, at least in part, accountable to others.

There is another similarity between these six conditions: in each case, we have made a deliberate personal decision. We choose to lust or choose, through an affair, to seek an end to loneliness or boredom. An important part of affair-proofing is quite simply this – it is making the choice not to. It is to recognise these conditions, see them as temptations and choose to reject them.

On their own – or even in combination – these conditions may not wreck a marriage. But to allow them to develop in a marriage is like leaving piles of highly flammable material lying around a home. You become a fire risk and you invite tragedy.

One final, but important point is that to allow these conditions to develop in your marriage not only makes it more likely that you will be tempted to have an affair, it also makes it more likely that your spouse will be so tempted. After all, when someone is too lazy to make a marriage work, it is not just them who may start looking around for pastures new, it may be their partner too.

I will return to the whole question of affair prevention in the next chapter. But first we need to look at the explosive issue of infatuation.

The Problem of Infatuation

Infatuation ('falling in love') has the ability to do wonderful, extraordinary and sometimes misleading things to our thinking. It was with good reason that our ancestors described infatuation as being shot by an arrow from the mischievous god, Cupid. Here, I want to look at an unfortunate aspect of infatuation, where one partner in a marriage suddenly finds, to their surprise or dismay, that they have fallen in love with another person. Suddenly, when they think of them it is as if a ray of sunlight comes into their brains, they cannot stop hearing their voice or imagining their face and they constantly long to be with them.

Infatuation is an astonishingly powerful, overwhelming and puzzling experience. It is so powerful that it can easily overrule reason and logic. Falling in love floods our thinking with emotions and causes our logic to short-circuit and switch off. We become 'fools for love'. It is this remarkable power that infatuation has of defying common sense which makes it so astonishingly dangerous in the context of affairs. In such a brain-fevered state, the most extraordinary actions suddenly become possible. You can have a man or woman with perhaps 25 years of unblemished, happy marriage behind them, who becomes suddenly infatuated with someone else and, within a matter of days, they can be seriously contemplating walking away from their home, spouse, children, friends and job.

When you flee temptation, leave no forwarding address.

If the conditions that I discussed in the previous section were like accumulating flammable items, then infatuation is like having a raging fire loose in your marriage. You have a major crisis on your hands.

Of course, the tragedy of infatuation is heightened because it is almost always a short-lived phenomenon. The result is that someone may let the fierce flames of an extra-marital infatuation burn out their marriage, only to find that this new relationship, for which they have forsaken all, loses its fire. But by now, it is too late to go back: all that they once had has been burnt to ashes.

Sometimes infatuation occurs where someone has consciously (or unconsciously) gone looking for it. Imagine, for example, that out of boredom, a man flirts with a woman he regularly meets as he commutes to work: he thinks of it as a bit of fun, something that livens up a dull journey. Then one day he realises that he cannot stop thinking of her, he is hopelessly involved emotionally and he realises that he is in love. His 'bit of fun' has triggered something far more serious than he could have imagined.

Yet if, in some cases, people go looking for infatuation, in other cases it comes to them. One day there is only respect, sympathy or admiration, the next day they are in love. This sort of 'accidental' infatuation is a real problem in the 'caring professions'. It is this, probably more than lust, which has wrecked the marriages of counsellors, teachers and even church ministers. But whether sought or unsought, if infatuation has occurred in a married person, then you have a problem.

Twelve warning signs of infatuation

Let me list a dozen of the early warning signs, which indicate that you are in danger of becoming infatuated with someone:

1. You find that you are sharing things with them that you do not share with your spouse.
2. You choose to spend excessive amounts of time with them.
3. You enjoy being with them more than being with your spouse and you feel excited about meeting them.
4. You feel that they understand you better than your spouse does.
5. You feel exhilarated or 'young again' when you are with them.
6. You take more care over your appearance when you meet them than when you are with your spouse.
7. You refuse to listen to warnings or advice about your relationship with them.
8. You feel defensive about the relationship so that you end up making excuses or justifying it using such phrases as 'she's really part of the family', 'he's going through some problems and I'm helping him' or 'it's purely a platonic relationship'.

When Mr and Mrs Henry Ford celebrated their golden wedding anniversary, an interviewer asked them 'To what do you attribute your 50 years of successful married life?'
'The formula,' Henry Ford replied, 'is the same formula I have always used in making cars – just stick to one model.'

9. You adjust your schedule or your travel arrangements so that you meet up with them, or – more seriously – so that you can meet up alone.
10. You find that, for no particular reason, you are thinking about them, and especially about their looks or charm.
11. You have fantasies – not necessarily sexual – about them in which this person replaces your spouse.

For instance, you imagine what it would be like to come home after work to be met by them.

12. You find yourself comparing your spouse negatively to them. You discover yourself thinking 'if only my wife had her charm and wit' or 'if only my husband had his good humour and looks'.

If these warning signs ever occur with any consistency and regularity then you are moving into dangerous territory. It is time to take action.

Five tools to handle infatuation

So what do you do to prevent Cupid's arrow of infatuation striking or, if it does, minimising the damage? Let me offer five suggestions.

1. Beware of the risks: remember, infatuation can wreck a marriage faster than anything can. Don't play around with emotions. Treat infatuation with the same respect that you would give a very large and very aggressive tiger at the zoo: don't try to open the cage and don't stick your hand in to stroke it. Remember too that just because what is going on between you and 'this special friend' is not sexual, doesn't mean it's all right. The exclusive intimacy of marriage is more than just sexual matters. The non-adulterous affair that I talked about earlier is still an affair and still breaks the exclusivity of the marriage bonds.

2. Take preventive action at the first hint of infatuation. If you sense even a faint dawning of an attraction to someone outside your marriage, the merest hint of a hormonal surge at their presence, distance yourself and quickly. Switch shifts, take a different train to work, ask your boss to relocate you

to your firm's Mongolian office – anything. But put miles between you.

3. Above all, don't act on your feelings. Being infatuated with someone who is not your marriage partner may not be wrong, but to act upon it is certainly wrong. Resist making matters worse, and remember that here, as elsewhere, adultery never ever helps matters. One problem today is that we have such a culture of sexual freedom that an intense emotional attachment can slide all too easily into a physical relationship.

4. If possible, take the matter to a trustworthy and reliable friend. I will discuss accountability later but in the case of infatuation, external help is vital. After all, infatuation is such an emotionally overwhelming experience that anyone suffering from it will find it very hard to make any rational decision about it. If you have an honest and accountable relationship with your spouse, then you may want to think about telling them. It may sound strange, and even possibly catastrophic advice to suggest that you tell your wife or your husband, 'Help, I'm infatuated with X!' or 'I feel I'm getting emotionally attached to Y'. But if your spouse is, as they ought to be, your closest friend, you may find it a big help. And anyway, they will probably suspect something soon enough!

No one knows us better than our spouse – and no one knows better the things we are in denial about.

David Stoop

5. One suggestion, which I would not restrict to Christians, is to pray. Be honest with God about the situation and ask him to strengthen you and to protect your marriage. It may be helpful to remember that although an infatuation for someone

other than your spouse can be an awesome emotional experience, in reality it is a temptation similar to the way that a desire to steal or to lie is. See it as a temptation and resist it.

Finally, remember that although infatuation is a high intensity experience, it tends to burn itself out within months. Hang on in there!

Chapter 6

How to Affair-Proof Your Marriage (2) Preventing Affairs, Crisis Management and Marriage Repair

After reading Jackie's letter, Nick realised that he could no longer avoid making a decision. He locked the door to his tiny, newly rented flat and walked thoughtfully down to the nearby park. Barely nine o'clock on a Saturday morning, the only people around were joggers and people walking dogs.

Nick noticed that the chestnut trees were turning brown and felt the crisp cool hint of autumn in the air. I used to enjoy this season, he thought sadly, remembering how the children had so reluctantly gone back to school and how, together, they had searched for conkers. He struggled against those memories, forcing them to one side. 'This morning,' he told himself, 'I have to sort out what I'm doing.' Jackie's letter with its offer of forgiveness and her wish to have him back had to be answered, and by this evening Sara would be back from the States. No, Nick decided, today's the day. I have dithered for too long: at this rate, I will have neither Sara nor Jackie.

He found a seat and sat down. Ahead of him the path through the park suddenly divided. How symbolic, he said to himself, that's where I'm at – the fork in the road.

He tried to grapple as coolly as he could with the issues. The choice was plain: Sara wanted him to make a clean break and get a divorce, and Jackie had made what was, in all probability, a final offer for him to return.

Nick sighed. Neither way was trouble free. To return to Jackie was to lose Sara and to suffer the humiliation of having to go back and start his marriage all over again. But, on the other hand, to choose Sara was no longer as attractive an option as it had been. The relationship with her had once seemed idyllic, liberating, and free from the constraints of marriage. Yet now, six months on, he had a growing sense of things closing in on him. There were issues that had to be 'formalised', Sara had said, and matters 'to be negotiated'. In short, and Nick felt himself smile ironically at the thought, the honeymoon was over.

Staring at the path branching ahead of him, Nick forced himself to think. 'How do I choose?' he asked himself, trying to weigh up all the issues.

Suddenly, Nick realised that he had made a decision.

He reached down deep into his pocket and found what he was looking for. How strange, he thought, that he had been carrying it with him. Had he subconsciously known what he was going to decide?

With a sense of urgency, Nick rose to his feet: there was a phone call to be made.

Putting the wedding ring back on his finger, he set off back to the flat.

Introduction

This second chapter on affair-proofing covers three topics. First, I want to look at how affairs can be prevented and then how, if they have happened, the crisis can be managed. Finally, I want to make some suggestions on the difficult and delicate topic of marriage repair.

Preventing Affairs

A lot of what has been written already in this book about building a strong marriage is relevant to affair prevention. Affairs are diseases of marriage, and those marriages that are strong and healthy have a much greater ability to resist them than those that are weak or sick do. Nevertheless, affairs are a potential threat to all marriages and I want to offer some specific guidelines on affair prevention. One thing to say at the start of this section is that, if you are married, you ought to put these suggestions in place now rather than later. It's a bit late to decide to change tyres when you are already in a skid. Once an affair has started, then you are no longer in the prevention business, you can only try to limit the damage.

Resolve to put your marriage first

In a number of places in this book, I have encouraged you to develop, extend and improve your marriage. I repeat that advice here; the very best defence against an affair is a vigorous, strong and valued marriage. It is easy to let a marriage drift, to be half-hearted about it, or just simply to think that it is good enough. I urge you to work at your marriage and not to be content with something mediocre. Quite simply, resolve that your marriage, not you, not your career, not your friends, nor your hobbies comes first. Not only that, but make it known that this is where your priority lies. Little things like putting a photo of your family on your desk at work make the point plain. It communicates to others that you are someone committed to your marriage and reminds you where your priorities and loyalties lie.

Recognise and act on the risks

Remember, the risk of your marriage breaking down is very real, so be on your guard. Increasingly in our culture, to be in a marriage is to take a stroll through a war zone. Be aware of your personal weaknesses and do whatever you can to protect yourself against them. In an age that encourages us to trust and affirm ourselves, we need to remember that the older and better wisdom was to be watchful of ourselves, aware that we all have the potential to choose the wrong path and to do wrong things.

Consider these illustrations of people who have recognised their own weaknesses and have resolved to deal firmly with them:

- A husband who, rather than be tempted by pornography when he travels alone during his business trips, hands over his TV remote control to the hotel reception desk.
- A woman who, when her husband is working away, refuses to read romantic novels.
- A man who, whilst having nothing against alcohol as such, never ever drinks when there is the possibility of any sort of sexual temptation.
- A businesswoman who has arranged with a few close, married, female friends that she can phone them at any time to talk through personal problems.

It is also important to realise that risks in a marriage alter with time. As a husband and wife mature and change as individuals, so does the relationship. For example, the difficulties and pressures of having young children soon change to the very different ones of having teenagers in the home. And as the relationship changes, so new weaknesses may develop and new risks surface. There is no guarantee that a couple who have a great marriage after five years will still have one after ten or twenty years.

Changing circumstances affect all marriages and set up stresses and strains that have to be dealt with. Some of these changes may be expected. For example, all long-term marriages will face the inevitable (but unpredictable) psychological and biological changes associated with ageing. Other changes may be brought about by events outside a marriage. For instance, think of a man who has been an active athlete, who has been running daily for most of his life and who sees himself as being someone who is fit and athletic. In his late thirties, he suffers an injury that damages a knee and the specialist's solemn verdict is plain – his running days are over. In a moment, his life has totally changed. Or imagine a woman who has always thought of herself as being beautiful, who has an accident that disfigures her. Can the dynamics of marriage adjust to handle these changes?

Changes, and the pressures associated with them, can arise from good events as well as bad ones. For example, think of a wife who is promoted to the position of senior personnel manager in her company. The extra salary and privileges are much appreciated, but with the promotion comes extra long hours, business trips abroad and heart-rending decisions on hiring and firing. Can the way her marriage functions adapt to handle these new stresses and strains?

The fact is that neither a marriage, nor the challenges

that a marriage faces are fixed and constant. Married life is like sailing down an unknown river: today you may be in calm, smooth waters, but there may be dangerous rapids just around the bend. There is no room for complacency.

See through the lies about affairs

One of the real dangers we face is that we believe the lies about marriage and affairs that surround us. Think of the television programmes or films you have watched recently. How were marriages portrayed in them? I suspect that, with few exceptions, they were shown as being dull, enslaving, cold, unstable and dead-end relationships. When did you last see a positive portrayal of a happy and passionate marriage on the small or big screen? Look through any collection of quotations on marriage and you will find that most of them are bitter and cynical. We are constantly being told that marriage is a doomed institution. The prevailing attitude is that you can try marriage if you want – just don't expect it to last.

The problem is that there are not only negative lies about marriage; there are also positive lies about affairs. In the media, affairs are portrayed as being happy, exciting, stimulating and rejuvenating. In affairs, sex is always breathless and passionate, while in marriages it is simply passionless. According to the media, to have an affair is a sign of maturity, of individuality, of liberty and of breaking loose from inhibitions.

Let me urge you to see through this misinformation, propaganda, lies, call it what you will. We cannot avoid the media's influence, but we can at least recognise how serious and distorting that influence is. You need to tell yourself again and again that this contrast of dull and oppressive marriages with exciting and fulfilling affairs is a total and complete lie. Yes, there are some lonely and awful marriages, but there are many more that are not. There are also many truly terrible affairs. In fact, all the research and all experience point to the same thing: affair-free marriages are generally happier, healthier, more stable and, in every way better than affairs.

Work at weaknesses

A lot of teaching on driving cars emphasises the value of defensive driving: of watching the road ahead and spotting hazards before they happen. Because no married couple can ignore the threat of an affair, there is a lot to be said for a similarly defensive approach to your marriage.

The fact is that any weakness in a marriage presents an opportunity for an affair to develop. This may sound obvious, but it is worth thinking about. You see it is easy to look over a marriage and say with quiet confidence that it seems to be 'in a good state'. Yet, a marriage that is in a good state generally, may still have a weakness that could allow an affair to develop. Think of marriage as a beautiful farmhouse, set amid fertile land on a flat plain, not far from a river. It is protected from the flooding of the river by four great embankments that form a great square around it. Well, it doesn't only get flooded when the water rises above the average height of the banks; it gets flooded when the water rises to the level of the lowest point on any of the embankments. Affairs can happen in marriages that are, on the whole, in quite a good state and even in those marriages that might be considered strong. Let me give you two examples:

- Rob and Mary have a marriage that works pretty well: there is sexual passion and a good deal of companionship and commitment. Privately, though,

Mary constantly criticises Rob and he feels undermined by her low opinion of him. Then, at work, he meets a woman who admires him and expresses her admiration for who he is.

> *You can bury a marriage with a lot of little digs.*

- Andy and Kate have a marriage in which there is nothing dramatically wrong, except that Kate finds her husband increasingly reserved, cold and joyless to be with. And among her colleagues, she is getting to know a man who is warm, witty and tender, and who listens attentively to her.

In both cases, the weaknesses of the marriage have allowed an opportunity for an affair to develop. In short, a marriage is only as strong as the weakest link. It is a useful discipline to look at a marriage and try to identify those areas where weaknesses exist. In previous chapters, I have talked about the various areas of a marriage where excellence was desirable. It is worthwhile thinking about those areas again to see how those dimensions of your marriage can be strengthened. And where you find weaknesses, try to work at removing or repairing them.

Look out for warning signs

The following are some telltale signs that all is not well between you and your spouse.

- You wake up still angry with them after a row the previous night.
- You don't spend as much time with them as you could.
- You make excuses to do different things to them.
- You wish you could spend more time away from them.

- You find some aspect of their personality repeatedly irritates you.
- You have regrets about marrying them.
- You accept the idea that your marriage is not going anywhere.
- You realise that you can't remember when you last laughed together.
- You find that some small weakness of your spouse is more important than their major strengths.
- You let secrets build up between you.
- You are aware that your only physical contact is driven by sexual desire.
- You realise that you can't remember when you last praised them, or they last praised you.
- You recognise that although you're married you still feel single.
- You decide that your marriage is something that you endure rather than enjoy.
- You find that you are saying harsh things about your spouse to your friends.
- You either use, or think, hard words about your spouse.
- You notice that one or both of you regularly dig up past failures in arguments.

Now, in most marriages some of these symptoms occur some of the time. But if a number of them occur frequently, then alarm bells should be ringing. You don't have an affair yet in your marriage, but you are in danger of creating conditions that are suitable for one.

If alarm bells do ring here, I suggest that you do two things. First of all, step back sharply from any relationship that is threatening your marriage. Take evasive action and dodge the threat. Second, try to sort out why this situation developed. Something somewhere is wrong. You may want to talk through what has happened with your spouse, a counsellor or a trusted friend. Your marriage has had a near miss and it would be wise to find what has happened and try to see how the weaknesses and dangers that have been revealed can be remedied.

Be accountable

To make yourself accountable is to put yourself in a position where you can be asked hard questions about what you are doing and why you are doing it. To be accountable is to be responsible for your actions. I suggest that there are four sorts of accountability: you can be accountable to yourself, your spouse, someone else, and to God.

Be accountable to yourself
To be accountable to yourself is to continuously examine what you are doing. It is to say to yourself, 'Should I be here?' 'Should I be doing this?' You can do this by setting limits: defining invisible markers or fences in your life to tell you when you are straying into dangerous ground and when immediate action is needed. For instance, how can you tell if a friendship is going too far? This is actually quite easy to answer. Ask yourself this question: 'If my spouse was here, would I have said or done what I did?' If a transcript or videotape of the meeting between you and your friend existed, could you hand it over to your spouse? If you couldn't, you have crossed the limit and it is time to act.

Be accountable to your spouse
It is important that a married couple have a strong degree of accountability to each other. There needs to be the

freedom for one party to ask the other the frankest questions and there needs to be the honesty for answers to be given to such questions. Now this is something that either needs to be introduced at the start of marriage or introduced gently – and with mutual consent – later.

Be accountable to someone else

Some people go further and say that it is good sense for each party in a marriage to have someone else, other than their spouse, to whom they are accountable. The idea is that each person in a marriage has a married friend of the same sex who they trust totally and with whom they regularly meet privately. At those meetings, the friend has a right to ask hard questions that must be answered honestly. So, for example, he might ask a husband about the state of his marriage and whether he was spending enough time with his wife.

There are many advantages of this sort of account-ability, in particular, the fact that this third party is distanced from the relationship and so can, in theory, offer impartial advice on how you and your spouse can resolve any issues. There are also risks. For one thing, because it involves at least a partial opening up of the privacy of the marriage to someone else, it is something that must be agreed between the husband and the wife. Permission to have this sort of accountable relationship cannot be taken for granted and there may need to be reassurances that the relationship is focused on accountability and not gossiping. The process of being accountable needs to be one that helps to defend, not destroy, a marriage.

Remember that, at your wedding, those present were called to be witnesses of your commitment to each other (and, if it was in a church, God). You are therefore accountable to them. They, in turn, ought to feel some responsibility for supporting you and you may find someone among them who will do their best to help you be accountable.

Be accountable to God

A fourth dimension of accountability is that which involves God. As a Christian, I believe that through Jesus we can know God as our heavenly Father and therefore come to him for help and support, knowing that he has a loving concern for us. Of course, being accountable to God is not a trivial matter. After all, I believe that God knows us far better than we know ourselves and we cannot disguise even our thoughts from him, let alone our words or actions. The idea that there is an unseen presence watching us is one that some people find hard to handle. Yet, we can't have it both ways. If you say that you like the idea that God is watching over you, then you can't logically complain about him seeing everything.

Crisis Management

And what if, after all, an affair – whether adulterous or not – is developing? I will talk about marriage repair in the next section. Here, I just want to say a few words to those for whom, for whatever reason, affair-proofing has failed, and who now find themselves in crisis management mode.

It is easiest here to address separately both of the parties in a marriage that has been affected by an affair: the one who is about to break their marriage vows and the one who feels that they are about to lose their spouse. Notice that I avoid using the words 'guilty' and 'innocent' here to describe these different situations. In reality, both terms may be appropriate, but in practice, they need to be avoided: the goal here is to prevent total disaster, not to apportion blame.

If it's you who is on the edge of an affair

If you are tempted to have an affair let me make five suggestions.

1. Respond decisively
I believe that marital disaster is only inevitable if you believe that it is inevitable. No adultery or affair automatically has to occur: the cry 'I couldn't help myself' is that of a programmed machine, not a human being. While there is still time, respond to the danger and act decisively.

2. Run from danger
The viewpoint of Holy Realism that I have put forward before holds, that while the temptation to have an affair can be resisted, it is nevertheless a real and powerful attraction that is not to be treated lightly. Avoid any possible dangers: never ever say of things like lust, 'Oh I can handle it.' Do not seek temptation and, if it approaches, run away from it. Against the enemy of affairs, it is the cautious, not the foolhardy, that survive to celebrate their golden wedding anniversary.

> *When we were married we made promises and we took them seriously. There've been a number of times in my marriage when – if I hadn't made promises I'd have quit – I'm not an easy person to live with.*
>
> **Madeleine L'Engle**

3. Resist fantasies
The root of adultery and affairs is the mind, so it is a wise rule to avoid fantasies. It is easy to assume that such a

rule applies only to those thoughts involving sexual athletics. Yet there are subtler and probably no less deadly fantasies: of starting all over again with him or her; of embracing and holding someone else; of driving off into the sunset together. Remember that from thoughts come actions. Resist such fantasies and reject them as soon as they arise.

Beware too of the fantasy of playing word games. It is all too easy to describe an affair as 'an adventure', 'a bit of something on the side' or even 'taking a holiday from marriage'. Be honest, call an affair what it truly is – a breach of marriage vows, cheating, breaking promises and above all, adultery.

4. Remember your promises

By entering into marriage, you have made a solemn covenant agreement with another person. Whether you should or shouldn't have done that is yesterday's problem, the point is you did. To break such a solemn promise is a very serious matter. If you brought God into your marriage vows, it is even more serious. Promises are meant to be kept.

5. Reflect on the cost

An affair may look very tempting. Yet if you can bring yourself to do it, take a piece of paper, make two columns on it and put down on one side all you would gain by your affair.

Having an affair is like taking all your savings and blowing them in a casino. You spend it all and you are quickly back to where you started. But a relationship is an investment.

And, as you look at that list, coldly ask yourself this: 'Are those gains guaranteed?' Can you be really sure that the affair you are about to embark on will indeed bring you what you seek? Are you absolutely positive that this relationship will not, in turn, go the way of the one you are about to desert? Then, in the other column, put down all the things that you would lose. In counting your losses, be honest: put down the hurts to family and friends, the financial and social costs, the damage to your reputation. Then ask yourself this question: 'Is it really worth it?'

If it's your spouse who is on the edge of an affair

You may not know all the facts, but you sense that disaster is looming. He or she is distant, withdrawn, preoccupied; there is a new coldness in your marriage. You feel you are about to be abandoned. You may even know who the other party is. So what do you do?

To be honest, this is such a difficult and painful situation that I barely feel able to offer counsel here, after all, anything I say could easily sound trite or facile. Yet, on the basis that some advice is better than none, let me make the following suggestions:

- *Don't panic.* This is a time for careful thought and action, not frenzied action or words. While calm may not save your marriage, you can be fairly certain that panic will not help at all.
- *Don't make things worse.* The temptation is obviously to summon up all the injustices and hurts that you have suffered and, with all the anger you can muster, tell your spouse what you really think of them. Whilst perfectly understandable, this is not helpful. In fact, your spouse may consciously, or subconsciously, be hoping for a major blow up so that you can take the blame for the marriage failure. A fire in a marriage needs to have sand or water put on it, not petrol.

- *Try to understand.* Try to work out the forces that are driving your spouse towards an affair. Even at this late stage, ask yourself if there is any action you can take to respond to these forces.
- *Ask if you must take any blame.* It is always easy to automatically think of oneself as the innocent party. Here you cannot afford that luxury – ask yourself whether you have contributed in any way to this situation. If you have, try to determine whether there is anything that you can do about it.
- *Try to communicate about the issues.* If possible, keep talking and make sure that the talking is a genuine two-way communication, not simply a way of fixing the blame or presenting your own position. In some cases, direct communication may be impossible: someone may be too badly hurt or too angry to talk, and in this case, you may need to find a counsellor who can act as an intermediary.
- *Try to agree to see a qualified marriage counsellor.* Counselling is no magical solution, but it is a great help. If your partner won't go, then go alone. Be prepared to forgive. I will talk more about the hard task of forgiveness in the next section, but in the meantime, try to put yourself in the frame of mind where forgiveness is a possibility.
- *Pray.* To any Christian involved in such a situation, prayer should be your first priority. Yet Christians sometimes need reminding that there is a God who hears and answers the prayers of his children. In your prayers, ask God to give you wisdom, guidance, peace and patience. Even if you are not a Christian, I would still encourage you to pray. You may be tempted to assume that God is unlikely to answer your prayer for help when you have neglected him for so long. But to do that would be to

limit God's mercy and love. Actually, many people have found that their first step to faith came in precisely this sort of a crisis. When you hit rock bottom, look up.

Marriage Repair

What if, in spite of everything, an affair happens? Clearly there is an obvious temptation to give up, to declare the marriage dead and to start thinking about a divorce. Yet, however tempting, such actions may be too hasty. Even at this late stage, it is possible that a marriage may be salvaged and repaired. Here I want to look at how, after an affair, a marriage can be repaired.

Let me make two preliminary points on marriage repair. The first point is to remind you that, as I discussed in the previous chapter, there are different kinds of affairs and they do different kinds of damage. Although serious, the non-adulterous affair – where someone has breached the psychological, social and spiritual bonds of a marriage, but not the sexual one – is probably much less damaging than an adulterous affair. And not all adulterous affairs do the same damage. The hurt inflicted on a marriage by a one-night encounter will probably be less than that done by the long-term affair, especially where it has been accompanied by lies.

The second point is to emphasise again that all affairs are serious. The possibility of marriage repair should not, in any way, be taken as an indication that an affair, even a non-adulterous one, is trivial. In marriage terms, you should consider an affair as being like a major car crash: always traumatic, often horrific and commonly terminal. It is a good idea to remember that the only guaranteed way for a marriage to survive an affair is for there not to be one in the first place.

Nevertheless, marriage repair is possible and an affair need not necessarily be the deathblow to a marriage. Probably more marriages than we imagine do survive affairs: after all, it's not something that any married couple ever boasts about. A marriage seems to be a fairly resilient social structure that is capable of surviving a lot of damage and which has the ability, under the right conditions, of healing its wounds. Of course, the state of the marriage is critical in determining whether or not it can survive an affair. The stronger the marriage (and, as I pointed out, affairs can occur in strong marriages), the more likelihood there is that there can be some sort of complete healing, although the wounds may be tender for years and the scars may never fade. However, in marriages that are already weak, an affair may just be the last straw.

In this section, I want to consider both those conditions that are essential for marriage repair and those factors that are helpful. As I discuss the important and delicate issues involved in marriage repair, I want to refer to a story that sheds light on the issues involved. Although I could invent one (after all, what does happen to Nick when he phones Jackie and what does Sara say when she gets back?), there is an already existing story that is even better for my purposes. It is a story that Jesus told of the lost son, sometimes called the Parable of the Prodigal Son, in Luke 15:11–32. It may seem an odd choice. On the surface, this story is about a rebellious son and how he is restored to his father, and at depth it is about how God treats those people who return to him in repentance. Yet it speaks strongly to marriages hit by affairs and in it we see, clearly and authoritatively defined, the basics of repentance and forgiveness.

The story begins with the breakdown of a relationship:

the younger son asks for his inheritance from his father and leaves him. In the close-knit society of that time, the son's actions would have been an appalling and very public insult to the father, effectively saying to him, 'I wish you were dead'. The parallels with an affair are striking: there is the same cruel shattering of an intimate and loving family relationship, the same public humiliation and the same sense of appalling loss. And doesn't every affair send the same terrible message to the abandoned spouse: 'I wish you were dead'?

As we look at the conditions for marriage repair, we will return to this story.

Two essential conditions of marriage repair

For there to be any repair or healing of a marriage after an affair, two conditions must be fulfilled: there must be repentance from the one who was involved in the affair and forgiveness from the spouse who they abandoned.

Repentance

The words *repentance, regret* and *remorse* are often used together here, but they mean different things and it is important to understand these differences. To *regret* something is to wish you hadn't done it, it is a thought, a verdict of the mind. *Remorse*, in contrast, is something that is much more an emotion: to have remorse is to feel a deep sadness and misery over what you have done. *Repentance* is more than each of these. It involves not just head thoughts or heart emotions, it involves a change of behaviour as well. At the heart of repentance is the action of turning back from what you have done or are doing.

Now these distinctions are important. While regret and remorse may be the starting point for repentance, they are, by themselves, an inadequate foundation for marriage repair. The fact is that because they do not necessarily involve a change in actions they may be temporary: the regret may simply be a short-lived verdict and the remorse may be just a brief emotional spasm. You can have both, but no real change. So someone in an affair may say, 'I feel regret about my marriage', or 'I have remorse over how I treated my spouse', but they may continue with the affair. Repentance, however, is something different. Someone who repented of having an affair would not just have bad feelings about their affair, they would give it up in such a way that it could never be renewed and they would return to their spouse with a genuine determination never to do it again. In the case of an affair, repentance would also involve looking carefully at how the affair happened and taking positive and decisive action to ensure that it could never happen again.

Initially, it is often hard to distinguish repentance from regret and remorse. Time, however, is the great test. While regret and remorse may be the decision or feelings of a moment, repentance proves itself over years. To repent of something, is to turn your back on it permanently.

Let me give two warnings. First, repentance must be unqualified. What I mean by this is that it is easy for someone to say that they repent of something and then to qualify that statement by adding something like, 'But, of course, what I did was understandable' or 'I was under stress' or 'It's the way I am' – by doing that, they undermine their repentance with excuses. An even worse strategy is to shift the blame. Here, the one who had the affair manages to make their spouse feel responsible. A typical example would be to say things like 'Of course, if you hadn't been so preoccupied at work . . .' or 'Well, you haven't exactly been sexually responsive lately'. True repentance doesn't offer excuses or seek to transfer blame. It simply admits guilt. Determining what went wrong and why can wait: repentance simply says, 'I'm really deeply sorry, it won't happen again' and means it.

Let's return to Jesus' story of the lost son in Luke 15. Far away from home, it all goes badly wrong for the rebellious son and, finally, hungry and in deepest misery, he resolves to return home with the following words: 'I will go home to my father and say, "Father, I have sinned against both heaven and you, and I am no longer worthy of being called your son. Please take me on as a hired man." So he returned home to his father.' Realising that he has forfeited the right of being called a son, he simply asks to be allowed to be a servant. This statement is a great summary of what repentance is all about. In it there is the admission of guilt, the acknowledgement of the hurts inflicted and the decision to return back, seeking nothing more than mercy. The son's sad walk home, rehearsing his confession as he goes, is a graphic picture of what it is to be truly repentant.

Forgiveness

Forgiveness is the counterpart to repentance and, unless both occur, a marriage cannot be fully repaired. I talked about forgiveness in Chapter 4, where I said that it was never an easy

Infidelities may be forgiven, but never forgotten.

option and this is certainly the case here. To offer forgiveness to a spouse who has abandoned you for an affair is one of the very hardest kinds of forgiveness.

The principles of forgiveness I discussed in the context of conflict resolution apply here, although, faced with all the hurts of an affair, forgiveness is even harder. In the specific context of marriage repair let me review the principles that I laid down there.

- *Forgiveness is the process where barriers of hate or guilt between people are removed.* Any affair creates an enormous amount of both hurt and guilt, and both of these have to be dealt with if there is to be any repair at all to the relationship. Unless these barriers are removed then there can be little hope of any intimacy being re-established.
- *Forgiveness is, first and foremost, a decision, not an emotion.* Because of the intensity and depth of the emotional hurt caused by an affair, it is vital to remember that at the heart of forgiveness is a decision and not an emotion. Even if we do not feel like it, we choose to forgive.
- *Forgiveness is not necessarily an instantaneous event.* This too is a principle that is highly applicable when there has been an affair. Forgiveness may be started in an instant, but it may only be fully achieved after years. In fact, time is such an important factor that I will talk more about it.
- *Forgiveness does not mean ignoring justice.* To forgive your spouse when they have had an affair is not to approve of what they did. It is not a case of saying 'It doesn't matter. I don't mind.' It is a case of saying (or at least letting it be understood) that it does indeed matter very much and you do mind, but in spite of that you have chosen to forgive. To water down, in any way, the wrongness of what happened would be wrong itself. It would also be unwise; it might increase the risk of it happening again.
- *Forgiveness does not necessarily mean forgetting.* In this context, this principle is of vital importance: you never forget an affair. It is actually easier to forgive strangers than friends or marriage partners. With a stranger, you may never have to see them again. In a marriage, there are constant reminders of what

happened. Nevertheless, despite such reminders, forgiveness means putting an offence or hurt behind you, so that it is no longer a barrier in the relationship.

- *Forgiveness should, ideally, be matched with repentance.* In the case of an affair, the response of repentance to an offer of forgiveness is vital. Someone may forgive their adulterous spouse, but they can hardly accept them back into the marriage unless there has been repentance. And, as I explained earlier, repentance is more than just feelings; it involves action. To repent of an affair would be to break it off and to genuinely resolve never to repeat it, or anything similar.

- *Forgiveness may be costly.* In the context of an affair, forgiveness may indeed be costly. Where the affair has been public, to take an erring spouse back can easily be seen as something pathetic – as an act of weakness.

Let me suggest that, in the context of an affair, there are at least two particular issues with forgiveness that ought to be noted. The first is that a single act of forgiveness may not be enough. The hurt of the forgiven affair may be like a weed: although you dealt with it, it may sprout up again and need further treatment. Months or years after you think the matter is closed, some new hidden and unresolved hurt to do with the affair may suddenly surface again. So, for example, imagine that Nick and Jackie in the story at the start of this chapter do indeed get back together, but that years later, he accuses her of not being committed to the marriage. Can you imagine the temptation for Jackie to snap back, 'Don't you talk to me about commitment – you're the one who walked out!' A further dose of forgiveness may be needed and both parties may need to be reminded that, once a matter is forgiven, it ought not to be re-opened.[1]

Another danger is that the partner who was abandoned may feel superior: after all, they stuck to the marriage. This problem is heightened by the gender differences that exist between men and women. So, for instance, a wife might completely fail to understand why her husband's sexual desires have drawn him into an affair. 'I would never do that,' she might say with contemptuous disbelief. Well, that is probably true, but if the temptation to have an affair had come to her in some other way, perhaps in the form of a man who respected and appreciated her in a way that her husband never did, would she have resisted? 'There, but for the grace of God go I' is not a phrase in the Bible, but it is, nevertheless, a very Christian attitude. No one can afford to feel superior. Yes there are innocent and guilty parties in affairs, but the moral gap between them may not be as big as some people think. And any expression of moral superiority may be extremely counterproductive.

Let's turn back to Jesus' story of the lost son, because at its heart lies the father's forgiveness. The story tells how the father, apparently watching out for the son, runs to meet him and embraces him. He cuts short the son's request to be a servant, restores him to his place in the family and orders a celebration. The father's forgiveness is not just loving, it is also costly. In that culture, the father would have been expected to punish the son for his wrongdoings and for the hurt that he had inflicted on his family. In restoring the son, the father lets himself be humiliated still further. This would be a powerful story if it were purely fiction. But because, in the character of the

---

[1] Of course, if someone who has been forgiven for something commits the same offence a second time, they are reopening the matter themselves.

father, Jesus is showing us what God is like, we see the standard set for what we ought to be like. This, Jesus is saying, is how we too should forgive. In fact, a third character in Jesus' story, the older son, highlights the generosity and cost of the father's forgiveness. Bitter and angry at what he sees as the injustice of the forgiveness, he refuses to accept the restoration of his brother. These differing attitudes of the father and the older son represent the two possible attitudes towards those who have broken their commitments, whether they are of sonship or of marriage. The wounded party has a choice: they can either offer forgiveness and restoration or judgement and rejection.

Be under no illusion – to offer forgiveness to an errant spouse is both hard and costly. It can be misunderstood, can be seen as a sign of weakness and comes with no guarantee of success. Yet, despite all the difficulties of forgiving someone who has hurt you so deeply, forgiveness is essential if a marriage is to be salvaged. Without forgiveness, repentance will achieve nothing and there can be no reconciliation. If you are not a Christian and face the issue of what to do with a spouse who has strayed, all I can do is suggest that you consider forgiveness as a strategy. If you are a Christian, then I have to say that, if you read the Bible, you will find that forgiveness is not just something that God suggests, it is something that he commands. Yet do not be totally overwhelmed by this demand: thankfully, through the Holy Spirit who is given to all who believe in Jesus Christ, God supplies the power to do those things he commands.

Three helpful factors in marriage repair

If repentance and forgiveness are the vital components to marriage repair, there are three factors that are helpful: time, effort and counsel.

Time

Although time alone does not heal a damaged marriage, it is a factor that aids healing. After an affair, marriage cannot be repaired overnight, even if there has been both true repentance

I cannot say whether things will get better if we change. What I can say is they must change if they are to get better.

G.C. Lichtenberg

and full forgiveness. An affair, especially an adulterous affair, breaks the bonds of marriage and they need time to grow back. In particular, trust needs to be re-established. For example, imagine an affair where a wife found out that her husband was inventing stories about business meetings in order to allow him to have liaisons with another woman. Even after the affair is ended and their marriage revived, it may take many years before she is totally happy when he goes away on business trips. Even when forgiveness and repentance have taken place, it is inevitable that there will be a sense in which the partner who strayed is 'on probation' for a long time.

Effort

All marriages require hard work, and when a marriage is bruised or wounded by an affair, this is even truer. When, with repentance and forgiveness, an affair ends, a marriage has effectively been given a second chance. It is a wise move to recognise this as a reprieve to the marriage and to use the opportunity to work at rebuilding it. While this idea of working at marriage is a general principle, there may also be some particular issues that need attention. One area of work might well include the causes of the affair. For instance, if lack of communication was a contributory factor, then every attempt should be made by both parties in the marriage to encourage discussion and sharing. Another area where work might be needed is on the effects of the affair. For instance, I believe that all affairs damage the self-esteem of the partner who has been abandoned. Once any affair is resolved, a lot of work will need to be done to restore their sense of self-confidence and self-worth.

Counsel

Look for 'Serious Internal Injuries' in any book of First Aid and, inevitably, you will read something like this: 'Seek expert help immediately'. Quite so! You don't do DIY on ruptured spleens or punctured lungs. In the same way, there is only a limited amount of self-help advice I can give on marriage repair. If things have gone as far as an affair, and especially an adulterous affair, then your marriage has suffered a serious internal injury and you are almost certainly going to need expert help from someone outside the marriage.

This need for some sort of external help is not simply because an affair is a very serious and complex injury to a marriage. It is because those in the marriage are generally too closely involved (or too traumatised) to be able to objectively assess the damage. The person who had the affair is probably too preoccupied with feelings of regret and guilt; and their spouse is probably busy struggling with their own feelings of hurt and anger. Someone external to the marriage, especially someone that is a trained counsellor, may be able to both identify the issues and suggest remedies. They may also be able to act as a neutral go-between or arbitrator in resolving issues. In other words, if you are trying to repair a marriage, try to find someone who can come alongside you and help.

Conclusion

Yes, affairs happen. They are a real risk to any marriage and especially to those marriages where the partners naively deny the possibility that they can happen. They are, however, not inevitable. Sensible preventative action, coupled with a firm and unshakeable commitment to make the marriage work, can help a couple survive the danger that they present.

And, if the worst does happen? Even then, the situation is not hopeless. With a willingness on the one side to make repentance, and on the other to offer forgiveness, a marriage may be repaired and restored.

Chapter 7

Looking Ahead – The Enduring Marriage

Edith was woken by the sunlight poking through the curtains. She turned and slowly squinted at her alarm clock and was surprised to find that it was only a quarter past six. 'It's nearly June,' she reminded herself, 'I shouldn't be surprised.'

For some moments, she lay back in the bed listening to Ben's shallow, unhealthy breathing next to her. She decided that she wouldn't go back to sleep and, slowly pushing aside the bedclothes, sat up stiffly. She swung her feet carefully out of bed and paused: she got dizzy if she stood up too soon. She turned to look at Ben, his face thin and pale, a strand of white hair adrift on the pillow. Edith reached out and touched his shoulder gently, as if to reassure herself that he was still there. Then she put her glasses on and cautiously got to her feet. Putting on her dressing gown and slippers she went to the kitchen and quietly made herself a cup of tea. Then she walked into the living room, drew the curtains and sat down in her armchair.

Sitting there in the early morning stillness, she looked around the room. They'd had the bungalow for what . . . 20 years? And yet this morning there seemed to be something about it that struck her for the first time. She found herself

186

noticing the ornaments and pictures. 'What a lot we've accumulated,' she thought and realised that she was not just thinking of the things but of all the memories linked to them.

The black and white pictures of the wedding. Edith shook her head. That had been 50 years ago. Next month would be the anniversary if . . . But Doctor Thomas had been hopeful that Ben would make it.

Other things caught her eye. The vase they had bought from Italy: that had been 1986. No, she corrected herself. Hannah had been fourteen, Edward twelve, so it was 1985. The photo of them all outside the old house, just before they moved. The children's photographs – school and graduation, Hannah's wedding to Brian, the grandchildren. The clock Ben had been given on his retirement. The painting they'd been given for their ruby wedding anniversary.

'Quite a little museum Ben and I have made here,' she thought. It was selective, she realised with a strange clarity – there was no evidence here of the struggles.

No memories of Ben's secretary – what had her name been? That had nearly caused so much trouble in the late seventies – but it had never come to anything. Or the arguments or rows they had had. She glanced at the dresser and felt herself smile: the dinner service was one plate short but no one noticed. Nevertheless, she shouldn't have thrown it. And what a joke, she couldn't remember now what the row had been about. But they had survived it all.

She sipped at her tea, oddly aware of her gnarled fingers. Her mother had never believed that the marriage would last, but it had. 'Well, Mum,' she said in her mind, 'we proved you wrong. Whatever happens now, whether or not Ben makes it through the summer, we are beyond all that. We have stayed together as we promised.'

'Nearly home,' she thought. 'Thank you God,' she said under her breath, 'thank you.'

In this chapter, I want to cautiously say a few things about what I call the 'enduring marriage': the marriage that has been tested and lasted for years. As a lifelong arrangement, there is no reason why a marriage cannot endure for forty or fifty years, or even more.

I only want to say a little about these enduring marriages for two reasons. The first is that if you think of marriage as being like a long cross-country hike, then I find myself writing about parts of the route that I, personally, have not travelled on. While that also applied to some of the issues to do with conflicts and affairs, there at least, I had the experiences of my contemporaries to draw on. Here, I am relying on information that comes from another generation. The second reason for brevity is that I am convinced that these long-term marriages basically draw on the principles that I have outlined in the previous chapters. For all the years they have accumulated, enduring marriages are fundamentally the same as newly-created marriages: the same rules apply.

> *Besides being a great way to exercise, walking together reminds us that marriage is a journey not a destination. It's a marathon, not a sprint. It's a lifetime union of two imperfect people who love each other.*
>
> **Claudia Arp**

That idea may seem surprising. I think this surprise is because our society thinks about marriage largely in terms of sexual activity and so tends to view marriage amongst older people as something totally different. Such a view is mistaken for at least two reasons. The first is, as I explained in Chapter 2, that contrary to widespread belief, an active sexual life can continue well into old age. Yes, sex in the later years of marriage may lack the frequency and fervour that it once had, but it is still there and it is still valued. The second, and more important, reason is that there is more to marriage than sex. The other bonds of marriage, those in the social, spiritual and psychological dimensions may, in fact, be strengthened with time: after all, by now the couple have been through a lot together. And, as I have pointed out repeatedly, there is far more to love than infatuation: enduring passion, as well as companionship, caring and commitment love, may persist and grow through the years.

The fact is that the same rules apply to a marriage in its fourth or fifth decade, just as they did during its first years. The challenges may be very different, but the principles stay the same. So the lessons learnt about communication, showing compassion, being sensitive about what you say and so on, maintain their importance over the years. In fact, it is in these latter years that the seeds carefully sown earlier in a marriage bear fruit. The hard work that went into resolving con-

> *An archaeologist is the best husband any woman can have: the older she gets, the more interested he is in her.*
>
> **Agatha Christie**

flicts, the efforts to ensure that there was effective communication, the grappling with the differing roles – all these things may show a real pay-off in later years. Conversely, it is at this time that the issues that were never resolved, but which were just brushed to one side, may return to haunt a marriage.

One key point that must be made is this: even a marriage that has survived thirty or forty years can still find itself in trouble. A particular danger of being in a long-term marriage is the danger of complacency; of thinking that now you are on the home straight. Surely, someone says, after so many decades, nothing can go wrong? After all, haven't all our struggles earned us a smooth journey, untroubled by rows and problems? Well, it would be nice to think that, after many years of hard work as a married couple, you could relax and enjoy the ride, but the reality is generally otherwise. The fact is that marriage break-ups and divorces occur even to couples who are in their sixties and seventies. All marital breakdowns are tragic, but the collapse of a marriage that has already endured for years is particularly sad.

Why, perhaps after three or four decades, does a marriage collapse? Let me cautiously suggest some reasons.

- A couple with a history of problems that were unresolved may have decided to stay married 'for the sake of the children'. Now, with the last child having left home, they find they have no reason to stay together.
- Another couple may have had major problems in their marriage that threatened to push them apart, but these were counterbalanced by strong sexual desires. Now, however, with waning libidos, the sexual side of their relationship is not enough to bond them.
- Yet another couple may have accumulated a large number of hurts and grievances over the years that they have never satisfactorily dealt with until, finally, something snaps. It is as if, whenever any conflict occurred, the issues raised were simply pushed into a mental cupboard and had the door closed on them. Finally, after many years, another totally trivial incident occurs. But now the cupboard is full, and when the door is opened all the accumulated hurts of the previous years spill out.
- In some cases, it may be retirement from work that causes problems. Imagine a dull and unexciting marriage, where for years the husband or wife (or both of them) found their stimulus and meaning in

their work. Then they retire and they are abruptly brought face to face with the empty void that is their marriage.

- Ill health may cause problems. For instance, think of a marriage where the main basis of the marriage has been weekends and vacations that centred on physical activities or sports. When, by virtue of age or ill health, one partner becomes unable to continue, the relationship will be affected by a major stress factor.

- An affair may occur. It is easy to think that affairs are threats only to younger marriages, and that long-established marriages have acquired some sort of immunity. The reality is that affairs can occur at any stage of a marriage. In fact, the attraction of an affair in later life may be heightened because of the way in which, with its excitement and hormonal stimulus, an affair promises to turn the clock back.

> *Let me not to the marriage of true minds*
> *Admit impediments. Love is not love*
> *Which alters when it alteration finds,*
> *Or bends with the remover to remove.*
> *O, no! it is an ever-fixed mark,*
> *That looks on tempests and is never shaken.*
>
> **William Shakespeare, Sonnet 116**

In the looming shadow of old age, such a promise of rejuvenation can be very tempting.

Let me make two suggestions to counterbalance the danger of complacency. First, remember to never ever take your marriage for granted. Always value your spouse. Second, see your marriage as a task or challenge that has been given to you to complete. Make it a matter of honour and pride to finish it well. Press on and be determined to finish the course.

Here, reluctantly, I need to raise an issue that is hard to discuss because our society tries to pretend that it doesn't exist. It is the subject of death. My reluctance to deal with this subject is heightened because throughout this book I have tried to find common ground between those who are Christians and those who are not. But faced with death there is no common ground: our perspectives are too different. And yet the topic of death cannot be avoided, because how we view our inevitable mortality greatly affects the later years of marriage.

Let me briefly try to express these differences. There are very few consolations to brighten old age for those people who do not have any certainty about a life after death. They may have more money, more time, and fewer responsibilities than they once had, but that is all. Although, quite understandably, they may prefer not to think about it, the fact is that their long-term future is at best cheerless, and at worst, terrifying. Realistically, the most optimistic view they can put on death is that it will bring them an end to pain and suffering. This gloomy and unavoidable prospect casts its shadow over all the joys of old age and can taint even its best moments. But for those who believe in Jesus Christ, the perspective is totally changed. Dying itself may still be unpleasant, but it is not now an end, it is instead a beginning. With the fear of death gone, the grave is simply a doorway through which the believer enters into the joy of being eternally present with Jesus Christ. This transformed view of death utterly changes the entire perspective on ageing for the Christian. The certainty that death will bring you into the presence of Jesus casts a bright light on even old age's

> *It is not darkness you are going to, for God is Light. It is not lonely, for Christ is with you. It is not unknown country, for Christ is there.*
>
> **Charles Kingsley**

most painful moments. With an increasing physical frailty, comes a maturing and a ripening. As the medieval alchemists dreamed of a substance that would change worthless lead to gold, so the Christian hope transforms old age. What others see as the glow of sunset, is for Christians that of dawn.

Let me say one final thing about these enduring marriages. We need to make an effort to honour those who have achieved many years in marriage because our culture unfairly overlooks them. In our age, the emphasis is placed far too much on the young and the beautiful. We need to redress the balance. There is something splendid about a silver-haired and wrinkled couple who have been faithful to each other for many years. They are the real heroes and veterans of marriage and we need to honour them and learn from them.

Chapter 8

Perspective

In these closing pages, I want to emphasise again four themes that have occurred throughout this book and which summarise its message. But before I do, I want to point out the need to think carefully through our views on marriage.

I have argued in this book that we live in an age where almost everything to do with marriage and love is the subject of confusion and misinformation. Our society holds out the vision of 'living happily ever after' in marriage, but says nothing about the ways to achieve the reality of a working and sustainable marriage. The views of marriage on offer are contradictory and oscillate wildly between Rosy Romanticism and Cold Cynicism, so that people are unable to decide whether to be married is to be part of a dream or of a nightmare.

Yet, the issue of marriage cannot go away. Every society, unless it is to collapse, must approve and endorse some stable social framework for men and women to live together and have children. Yet, despite endless efforts, no real alternative has been found to the traditional marriage pattern of one man and one woman committing themselves totally to each other for life. All other options either fail to provide stability or, more worryingly, penalise either the women or children involved. Of course, the virtue of the traditional marriage is not because it is traditional, but because it was created on the principles laid down in the Bible.

I do not believe that it is enough to simply call out for a return to traditional marriage. Putting the clock back is far too simple a solution. Instead, I think we need to do some hard thinking about what a marriage really is, what it stands for, and how we can best make our marriages work. The answers, and the message of this book can, I believe, be summarised in four simple commands: understand marriage, understand love, be fully committed to marriage and be encouraged about marriage.

Understand Marriage

We have seen that in our society there is enormous and widespread confusion about what marriage is. The result is that many people who decide to get married have no real idea about what a marriage entails and what they are agreeing to. In view of the inadequate appreciation of the nature of the commitments that a marriage requires, it is hardly surprising that so many marriages fail.

Anyone who is married or even considering marriage, should try to grasp something of the reality of what marriage is all about. Let me again give my definition of marriage: 'a legally recognised, lifelong union between one man and one woman involving psychological, sexual, social and spiritual bonds'. This definition is no personal novelty: all it says can be found in the Bible, and is either stated, or implied, in the wording of the nearly five hundred-year-old traditional marriage ceremony.

To truly understand marriage is to comprehend the all-embracing scope of what is involved. It is not just a sexual or social linkage between a man and woman; it is something far richer and more extensive and involves all the four main aspects of separate dimensions of life. Psychologically, a marriage involves an intense companionship based upon sharing and intimacy at the deepest possible levels. Sexually, a marriage involves mutual sexual desire, and its expression in activities ranging from hand-holding to sexual intercourse. Socially, a marriage involves a couple becoming one, and the creation of a totally new family unit. Spiritually, a marriage involves a commitment to share those beliefs upon which we focus our hopes and base our lives. The task of a married couple is to unite as deeply as possible in the psychological, sexual, social and spiritual areas of life. Yet their task is more than this: it is not just to create bonds in these areas; it is also to create boundaries in them. A married couple need to define limits in these four dimensions that protect their exclusive intimacy with each other.

To comprehend marriage though, is not just to understand its all-embracing scope, it is also to understand its duration. The deep intimacy of marriage can only be created when there is a solemn promise that these bonds and boundaries will be maintained for life. The promise of commitment 'until death us do part' is not wishful thinking or an optional extra, it is an essential precondition for the intimacy of a marriage.

Understood this way, a marriage is a far more extensive and challenging undertaking than our bewildered society today generally assumes. To agree to marry someone is not just to agree to move in with them, or even to share bank accounts: it is to make a commitment to be united with them in every dimension of life.

Understand Love

If there is any agreement at all on marriage today in our society, it is that love is involved: the problem is that no one seems to know what love is. The general perception is that love is some sort of mysterious emotion; an irresistible and irrational feeling that descends on people without warning. How this love specifically relates to marriage is problematic: after all many people who claim they married for love end up seeking a divorce on exactly the same basis.

The reality is that just as our culture has an incomplete understanding of marriage, so it also has an incomplete understanding of what love is. These 'falling in love' feelings are indeed part of love, but only a small part. As we saw, there are four types or forms of love: craving, companionship, caring and commitment love. When people fall in love they experience only the most spectacular form of craving love. This limiting of love to a stunning, but often short-lived emotional phenomenon is not just a matter of poor psychology – it is a mistake that is potentially catastrophic for marriage. On such a view, love cannot be commanded, it can only be experienced, and to base a marriage on this is to stake everything on moods and feelings.

The fact is that the other forms of love: companionship, caring and commitment love, are acts of the will rather than the emotions. Craving love for another person cannot be ordered, but we can make ourselves have companionship love by choosing to show someone friendship and interest, and can make ourselves have caring love by choosing to show someone compassion. In fact, commitment love is purely and simply the decision to keep our promises to support someone whatever happens. Not only then, is this fourfold love far broader and stronger than popularly imagined, it is also more permanent. Yes, there is an emotional component to the love that a marriage requires, but there is also a high degree of decision, commitment and determination to it. This sort of love can be both demanded and promised.

To understand love this way is to transform a marriage. We do not leave our partners because we have fallen out of love with them and fallen in love with someone else; we stay with our spouses because we have made a commitment to love them. Love is not just a feeling to be felt, it is a command to be obeyed

Be Fully Committed to Marriage

To understand both marriage and love is vital, but understanding is not enough: there must be a full commitment to marriage. I characterised the two main views on marriage today as Cold Cynicism and Rosy Romanticism. The Cold Cynic assumes that a marriage will fail; the Rosy Romantic that it will automatically succeed. Neither view encourages a full commitment marriage.

This call to be fully committed to marriage is the challenge to commit everything you have towards its success. To be married is like diving into a swimming pool: the only way to do it is to do it wholeheartedly. What such a full commitment means will vary from marriage to marriage. In one marriage it may be seen in someone's costly resolve to stay with a spouse who is chronically ill; in another it may be seen in the giving up of a promotion because of the way that it would encroach on the marriage. This commitment is full, not just in how much it commits, but in how long the commitment lasts for. To be fully committed to marriage is to make the commitment open-ended; it is to remove any time limit to your promises.

The call to be fully committed to marriage does not, however, stop at our own marriages. It is the challenge for all of us, whether married or not, to support practically, the marriages of our friends, neighbours and relatives. It is also a challenge to support the whole idea of marriage in our society. Marriage is

My most brilliant achievement was my ability to be able to persuade my wife to marry me.

Winston Churchill

under threat from the scorn of those who have rejected it and the hurt scepticism of those that have tried it and found that either marriage failed them, or they failed it. Widespread cohabitation undermines the foundation of marriage, and easy divorce the idea of its permanence. Both the principles and the practice of marriage need to be defended.

Christians who are married should see in their marriages something of special significance. To achieve a successful marriage is pleasing to God: indeed, we can consider it part of our worship of him. Yet our marriages are not just part of our worship, they are perhaps the greatest test of who we are. Here, in the daily, intimate encounters with our spouses over many years, we see the rigorous testing of who we really are, and are given the opportunity to demonstrate our faith in word and deed.

Marriage requires our fullest and most complete commitment; it needs all we can give it.

Be Encouraged About Marriage

Yes, marriage is a challenge. Indeed, most of us will face no more demanding a task in our lives than making a marriage succeed. And it is easy to be daunted about marriage: we all know marriages that have failed spectacularly and painfully. For two people to be bonded permanently together through sickness and health, poverty and riches, joy and sorrow seems an almost unattainable goal.

In the face of this daunting challenge, let me offer three encouragements.

The first is this: success in marriage is well worth seeking. Despite the fact that our jobs may dominate our lives, our successes and achievements in the workplace are likely to be short-lived triumphs. Who, in twenty years' time, will remember that you were the one who successfully negotiated some contract or pushed your firm's third-quarter sales figures to a new high? In contrast, our achievements in making a marriage work and creating a stable, friendly and hospitable home will have results that will echo on through children and friends for many years to come. Marriage is worth the effort.

The second is that God has given us all the capacity for marriage. This is not to belittle the single state, whether that occurs by choice or by necessity. But it is to say that marriage is not some bizarre and impossible social structure, imposed on human beings by an accident of history and sociology: it is something that, whether we are Christians or not, we were made for.

The third encouragement is specifically Christian. It is that God cares about our marriages and desires to help us. The Bible teaches that if we come to God humbly (and there is nothing like marriage for developing humility), confessing our mistakes and regrets and putting our trust in Jesus Christ, then God will come alongside us and strengthen us through his Spirit. God delights to forgive, restore and to supply the resources for our needs. I am encouraged when I read, in chapter 2 of John's Gospel, that Jesus' first miracle was at a wedding where the festivities were in trouble. He has been helping marriages ever since.

Does marriage really work? My answer is that I believe it does, because it is God's invention and not ours, and that the same God who made marriage is still present and available to help those who determine to practise it!

Bibliography

Arp, David and Claudia, *The Second Half of Marriage* (Zondervan, 1998)

Bloomsbury Biographical Dictionary of Quotations (Bloomsbury, 1997)

Dickens, Charles, *David Copperfield* (Penguin Books, 1994)

Encarta® Book of Quotations (Microsoft Corporation, 1999, 2000)

Jaquette, Dale, *Philosophical Entrées: Classic and Contemporary Readings in Philosophy* (McGraw-Hill, 2000)

Journal of Family Psychology (APA Journals, 1999)

Lahaye, Tim and Beverley, *The Act of Marriage: The Beauty of Sexual Love* (Zondervan, 1998)

L'Engle, Madeleine, *A Circle of Quiet* (HarperCollins Publishers Inc., 1972)

The Oxford Dictionary of Quotations (© Oxford University Press, 1999)

Small, Dwight H., *After You've Said I Do* (Fleming H. Revell Company, 1968)

Stopes, Marie, *Married Love* (Hogarth Publishing, 1918)

Stoppard, Dr Miriam, *The Magic of Sex* (Dorling Kindersley, 2001)

Welwood, John, (ed.), *Challenge of the Heart* (Shambhala Publications, 1985)

Wheat, Ed and Gaye, *Intended for Pleasure* (Scripture Union, 2000)

Other Books on Relationships by J. JOHN

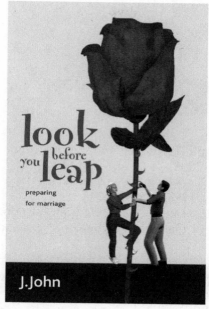

We are constantly being told that marriage is a doomed institution. The prevailing attitude is that you can try marriage if you want – just don't expect it to last.

Popular speaker J. John has written *Look Before You leap* because he believes that marriage *does* work and he wants to help make it work for others too.

In *Look Before You Leap* J. John demonstrates the foundations required to build a healthy marriage that will work.

Specifically he covers the following areas:

- What marriage and love are all about.
- Singleness.
- The delicate issues of dating.
- The alternatives to marriage.
- The awesome seriousness of making *that* decision.

Whether engaged or contemplating marriage this book, with its thoughtful and witty, down-to-earth wisdom, is for all those thinking about getting married.

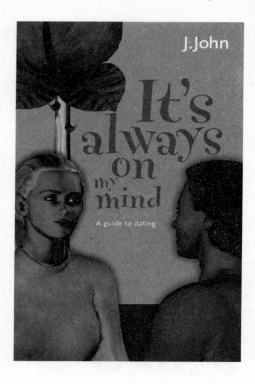

It's always on my mind

A guide to dating

J.John

Love, sex, being single, relationships, guilt, why wait and finding the right partner are all issues faced in this revised edition of this J. John classic.

It's Always on My Mind has been written because the majority of people find that their expectations of love, sex and relationships frequently occupy their attention.

Images of sex are everywhere. From TV advertising to teen magazines, we are confronted by literally hundreds of images a day being used to sell us everything from cars to coke.

At the end of each chapter there is a 'Take it Further' section, to help the reader think through the issues raised. There are suggested passages from the Bible to read and study, and talking points for discussion. The action section is subdivided, giving different suggestions for those still at school, those still single, and those engaged or nearly engaged.